Wanderlust
and lipstick

The Essential Guide
for Women Traveling Solo

The Essential Guide
for Women Traveling Solo

Beth Whitman

PO Box 16102
Seattle WA 98116
www.dispatchtravels.com

*Wanderlust and Lipstick: The Essential Guide for
Women Traveling Solo*
©2009 by Beth Whitman

Published by:
Dispatch Travels
PO Box 16102
Seattle, WA 98116
www.dispatchtravels.com

ISBN 10: 0-9787280-6-8
ISBN 13: 978-0-9787280-6-9

LCCN: 2009922559

Editor: Leslie Forsberg www.leslieforsberg.com
Illustrations: Elizabeth Haidle www.ehaidle.com

Purchase additional copies online at:
www.wanderlustandlipstick.com.

Printed in the U.S.A.

For the intrepid women who have gone before me,
in life and in travel

CONTENTS

INTRODUCTION

As the 2nd edition of this book goes to print, much has changed in the last two years.

Predictably, the Internet has continued to explode, leaving few stones unturned around the world. It has connected people—through forums, social networking sites, and blogs—from the farthest reaches of the Earth. Tibetans are in conversation with Americans and Indians are befriending Germans, all through the technology. They're sharing sightseeing tips, a cup of coffee, and their homes.

Yet in the business of travel, an industry that has seen (and relied upon) growth year after year, even a slight decline has had a deleterious effect. While many of us globetrotters have been busily getting to know each other through Twitter and Facebook, the rest of the world appears to be in freefall: airlines are struggling to stay afloat; occupancy rates at hotels are at record lows; restaurants and shops are closing; publishers have postponed publication of some guidebooks.

I might live in a travel bubble. Few, if any, in my community have curbed their plans to set out on an adventure. Rather, they are cutting back on holiday and home spending and channeling their money into longer trips and journeys of their own, whether a destination birthday trip or their dream adventure.

And, we women continue to lead the way, having found the courage to set out on our own. It's become acceptable, almost fashionable, to take time for ourselves. We're backpacking our way through South America, taking yoga classes in India, and making our way to the top of the Eiffel Tower to fulfill a life-long wish.

I've never received so much feedback from women that they *need* to travel *now*: as an escape, a lifestyle change, or a mental health break. One of my friends travels each year without her husband and young son to give herself a break from daily responsibilities. "Happy wife, happy life," she says, grinning from ear to ear.

Whatever your reasons, don't hesitate another moment to nurture your inner Wanderluster!

Travel Well!

Beth

1.

WHY TRAVEL SOLO?

IN *my many years of teaching workshops for women travelers, I have come into contact with both the courageous and the timid who are interested in traveling on their own. Whether they are fresh out of college, in a healthy marriage that encourages independence, newly divorced, widowed, or have simply found the motivation to take the next step, it's clear that they are not waiting to find the perfect travel partner before making plans. Now it's your turn.*

Perhaps you wonder what benefits solo travel can offer you, how it differs from traveling with a tour group or with friends. Consider some of the following advantages of traveling solo.

✤ Freedom

As a solo traveler, you're the boss. No coordinating agendas, no arguing over where to eat and when, no wasting time visiting attractions that don't suit your interests. You can sleep late, skip breakfast, take an earlier train than planned, stop for photos along the way, or duck into a movie theater to see the latest movie dubbed in the local language. No negotiating or compromising with anyone.

While it can be a relief to leave the travel planning to others so you don't have to think beyond your morning croissant and coffee, you often give up what you really want to do when your tour director or travel mates make the decisions.

Wayward Women is a loose-knit group of women travelers that meets monthly to talk about travel. Jo, the co-creator of this Seattle-based organization, loves being able to do things her own way. "I don't travel with others because it means I'd have to make compromises in terms of where I'm going and how long I'm staying. At the national museum in Wellington, New Zealand, I was the first one there in the morning and the last one to leave at the end of the day. I would have been annoyed if I had had to compromise."

On a recent trip to Europe to study chocolate making, Mary Jo admits it would have been nice to have her husband there, but, "I enjoyed being alone because it really allowed me to focus on the work I was doing."

You'll be More Approachable

You'll meet far more people when you're on your own since you won't be insulated as part of a couple or group. Having even one travel partner makes it intimidating for others to chat you up. As a solo woman, friendly encounters with other travelers and locals abound, and you might even be the recipient of romantic advances.

Laura has traveled the world on her motorcycle, with group tours and as a solo rider. "When I travel alone, I meet new people. I don't shut them out while talking to a friend."

For better or worse, as a stranger in a strange land, be it a New Jerseyite in Alaska or a Canadian in Argentina, you're most likely going to stick out. You'll be a curiosity, and people will want to talk with you. They may provide you with directions if you're poring over a map, or invite you to dinner so that their family can practice English. Or they may simply visit with you to pass the hours on a long journey.

No matter how introverted you may think you are, we all need to reach out and talk with others. You could very well find you are more outgoing and likely to approach others than you ever thought you could be. As a result, solo travel is rarely lonely.

Finding Your Strength

Yes, it does take more emotional and physical energy to travel solo. You'll need to be hyperaware of your surroundings to overcome challenges and avoid dangerous situations, all the while being responsible for your personal possessions. These hassles pale, however, in comparison to the rewards.

When you're the only one in charge of your travel, you learn to handle situations and be strong. Once you've come out the other side of a challenging experience, such as getting lost on the Mexico City Metro or getting food poisoning while on a trip to Denver, you'll realize there are few things you can't handle, and you'll have an overwhelming sense of accomplishment.

Susan packed up her things after her divorce at age 31 and traveled the back roads of the United States in her camper van for a year. Her three rules were: Never drive at night. Never drive more than 200 miles in one day. And never take an interstate. At one point early in her travels, she suddenly realized she was really on her own. "I pulled the car over, put my head on the steering wheel, and had to pump myself up and say, "I can do this."" Suffice it to say, she did it and more. Twenty-five years later, she's guided tours around the world, lived in Bangkok teaching English and kayaked the coast of Chile by herself for three months.

Having Peak Experiences

In his book *Flow: The Psychology of Optimal Experience*, psychologist Mihaly Csikszentmihalyi refers to flow as the time when you become lost in your actions, whether climbing a mountain peak, painting or playing soccer. The late actor Spalding Gray called it "the perfect moment."

Call it what you will, but many find it in travel. It's the peak experience or string of events you encounter when you're open to new sights, sounds, and smells. The universe works with you. The right people show up when you want to share the expenses on a tour. You're invited to dinner at a stranger's home just when you're feeling the most homesick.

౫౫౫ Erin's Story ౫౫౫

I had taken a cruise with my mom, brother, and aunt, and that's what sparked my interest in wanting to travel. I had become friends with some of the crew members, and one night a guy and girl from Romania invited me out on the deck. We talked all night and I learned about their culture and about working on the ship. Sitting on deck and looking out at the ocean made me realize there was a big world out there that I hadn't experienced.

My dad had passed away a few years earlier, and I realized that life was too short to not take chances.

I had always been terrified to fly, but I got a job interview for a cruise line and had to fly to Miami from Seattle. I knew if I didn't do it, I would always regret it. I got the job!

I was sent to France for the launch of the ship. I had been sheltered growing up, and had never before left the United States. I was feeling anxious about leaving the country by myself. I knew it could take me awhile to cope with things, but here was the chance for me to be an independent person.

It's interesting what fears you're willing to overcome to manifest what you truly want in life!

To be by myself made all the difference in the world. I learned to be concerned about the things that were important and not worry about the smaller details. I'm a different person now because of the experience. I find I am more comfortable with doing things solo—from eating out at a restaurant to strolling through the park.

Today, I am less inhibited because I traveled alone, and my experiences abroad now infuse my daily life.

When traveling with others, peak opportunities don't present themselves as readily, and/or you simply may not be as aware of these unique moments. Coleen, who lived in the south of France for six months, knows how distracting it can be when you're with other people.

"When I'm alone, I absorb the experience 100 percent. It's more raw. When I travel with other people, I miss stuff because I'm talking to them or they're in a bad mood. If they're in a bad mood, you can miss a whole day."

Maricris spent two years working in London and came to expect these peak experiences during her European travels.

"Everyplace I went, I knew there would be a time when I had a 'wow' moment and would say 'I can't believe I'm doing this.' The very first 'wow' moment I had was in the Loire Valley in France. I was walking up a long path with tall trees. Fallen leaves were covering the path. The castle was like from a fairy tale, and I wished that my niece was there so she could see that castles do exist."

Like Maricris, it's because of these peak moments that I'm addicted to travel. I keep going back out into the world for the sheer joy of these heightened experiences.

2.

TRAVEL IDEA GENERATOR

THERE'S *taking a trip. And then there's creating a journey that awakens your senses
and changes your life. The very nature
of travel, in which you are thrust into a different
environment, causes you to see the world in new
ways. Following your dreams and interests and
then putting a plan into action can help you create
a purposeful and rewarding adventure.*

✤ What's Your Purpose?

Planning your travel around a favorite hobby or interest can give you a sense of purpose. As a music fanatic, I search whatever location I'm in for the best local (non-chain) music store for instruments and local music so I can bring home a fabulous souvenir that I'll enjoy many times over.

If you love to cook, look for a regional or local restaurant cookbook. For a more active experience, join a dance class that emphasizes the region's specialty, or take a class in the local language.

What engages you and gets you excited in your everyday life? Take that interest and apply it to your travels. In doing so, you'll already have a certain level of comfort and confidence, and immersing yourself in a new environment will open you up to a new view of the world.

Regardless of what you do, consider how you'll do it: as an adventure trip, a soft adventure, or perhaps a relaxing getaway. Mix, match, combine, stir, and enjoy!

✤ Adventure Travel and Soft Adventure

Adventure travel is often associated with thrill-seekers, and generally requires more stamina and participation than your typical vacation, as it tends to include physical activity. This type of travel is often done in more remote regions. While adventure travel may sound risky to some, to those who are fitness buffs or outdoor lovers, this may be the perfect way to experience a new place.

Think: climbing peaks in Colorado that are over 14,000 feet high or bicycling the back roads of Germany's Alps. Whether it's in relative comfort or you are on a shoestring budget, adventure travel should leave you exhilarated and perhaps exhausted. (Those sore muscles mean you completed something worthwhile.)

If you are setting out on a truly adventurous journey, you'll need to be better prepared than a Boy Scout in the woods. Susan, who spent three months paddling her kayak off the coast of Chile, said she had to "figure out what would kill me" and then planned for it. What was she most concerned about? "Rolling the kayak and not being able to right it."

Susan notes that she is more cautious when she's on her own and, as a result, she never puts herself in situations that would be considered dangerous.

Soft adventure (also called experiential travel) gets you close to (and sometimes involved with) the culture, wildlife, and nature—with less sweat. This sort of travel is a great way to experience a region without stepping too far out of your comfort zone.

Soft adventure may include easy hikes to birding locations, viewing the crashing glaciers of Alaska's Prince William Sound from a tour boat or joining a safari tour. Experiential trips also encompass learning about the local culture through classes or workshops. These experiences can range from cooking classes to photography workshops to architectural tours.

Hiking—Hiking allows you to experience the landscape and wildlife, and even the local communities, up close. If you enjoy the outdoors, hiking can be an affordable way to explore a new place. You can do everything from urban walks to day-long or week-long trips on trails, or even navigate through an entire country.

Europe has an extensive system of trails that flow from country to country, as well as urban walks in numerous cities. You

Plan Your Hike

Several organizations can help you plan your adventure. Start your research with Trails.com (www.trails.com). This website includes extensive information and topographical data on hiking trails throughout the United States, Canada, Mexico, and the Caribbean. There is a membership fee to access their maps, but you can check it out with a 14-day free trial.

Also visit the American Hiking Society (www.americanhiking.org) website, which lists local events and volunteer opportunities, in addition to trail information.

Traveling to Europe? The European Ramblers' Association (www.era-ewv-ferp.org) maintains 11 long-distance paths across Europe. Their site includes trails in 27 countries, from Austria to Slovenia, and has a comprehensive list of contacts for each nation.

can hike between diverse regions and experience a variety of languages and landscapes from one day to the next. For a unique experience, you might consider traversing a well-worn pilgrimage path, such as the Camino de Santiago, in Spain.

New Zealand is one of the best-known countries for tramping, as the Kiwis call it. With rugged mountains and volcanoes to stunning beaches, it's no wonder that tramping is their most popular outdoor activity.

Asia and the Indian subcontinent are recognized for some of the most popular and breathtaking hikes on the planet. You can choose from relatively easy treks through rambling hillside towns, to high-elevation climbs, such as those in the Himalayas.

Wherever your travels take you, you'll need to make sure you're walking into a stable political situation. Use common sense.

In more remote regions, uprisings and civil unrest change constantly. As a solo traveler, talk with others and participate in online forums or blogs (both are discussed in Chapter 4, Mapping Out the Details) for input from those who've recently traveled to the region. If going solo isn't safe, then sign up with a tour company that specializes in hiking.

Biking—While packing up your bike poses a bit more of a challenge than packing a pair of hiking boots, there's nothing more exhilarating than meandering through the French countryside on a bicycle or maneuvering through the crowded streets of India.

Biking on your own is an affordable and flexible method of travel. While you'll need to take riding gear, such as a helmet, gloves, specialized clothing, and panniers, you won't have to pay for trains, buses, or taxis (unless transporting your bike between points), and you won't have to rely on a mass-transit schedule.

Some of the more popular biking destinations include the United States (particularly the Northeast and the West Coast), New Zealand, Italy, France, and Ireland, but the beauty of biking is that it can be done anywhere.

If you like the idea of bicycle touring, but don't feel comfortable handling all the logistics by yourself, some tour companies offer self-guided tours in which you set the pace but they handle meals and hotel bookings on your behalf. And, of course, many tour companies have organized group tours. Either way, support vehicles are used in case any mechanical or physical issues arise.

While there are literally hundreds of bike tour companies to choose from, you'll find that some offer more than the usual tour. DuVine Adventures (www.duvine.com), for instance, offers trips that incorporate yoga. Ommmm.

To learn more about biking the roads of North America, visit the Adventure Cycling Association website (www.adventurecycling.org).

Prepare for your trip by building endurance and strength during the months and weeks leading up to your adventure. Know the terrain you'll be encountering. Will you be on dusty dirt roads, rambling mountains, or city streets? Tune up your bike and become educated about fixing flats and addressing gear issues, as well as handling chain and brake problems.

If you aren't setting out directly from your home, you can ship your bike to your destination by using a pre-made bicycle box from CrateWorks (www.crateworks.com), or you can ask your local bike shop to handle the shipping. Airlines will charge you an additional luggage fee, which varies from airline to airline. Railways and buses may charge extra, as well.

Alternately, you could rent a bike or, for a longer trip, buy one at your destination and then resell it once you've completed your journey. The downside is that these bikes may not be as comfortable as your personal bike (although you could always bring your own bike seat), but it does make getting to your starting point easier when you don't have to carry or ship your own bicycle.

Outdoor Recreation—One surefire way to stay in shape during your vacation is to pursue opportunities to participate in your favorite outdoor sport, such as windsurfing or golf, and center your days around being active. As a woman traveling on your own, you'll likely meet others who are involved in the same activities, instantly expanding your network of companions.

Bringing Your Own Gear

Start a list well in advance that includes the accessories you'll need. Browse shops or online stores that specialize in gear for your interest. You might find some items you weren't previously aware of that could make your trip easier, or it might jog your memory as to some other things you nearly forgot to pack. You may intentionally leave bulkier items at home and do without or rent them once you've arrived. While planning a snorkeling trip to Baja, Mexico, for instance, I chose to not take flippers due to their bulk, but instead, took my own mask and snorkel.

Take extra precautions once you've arrived. You'll be in unfamiliar territory, perhaps trying out a new air tank or an untried surf spot. Ensure that your gear is in good working order and, if possible, buddy up with someone so you can watch out for each other.

If you don't already participate in a sport but want to learn, plan to take lessons before you leave. Sometimes, however, options at home may be difficult to come by. If you live in Indiana and have always wanted to learn to scuba dive, your options may be thin. But head to Belize and you'll be overwhelmed by opportunities to receive your diving certification in the country's ever-changing underwater marvels.

❧ Group Tours

If you are pressed for time, you can easily see a large number of sites within a city by joining a group tour. An organized tour can also help you reach areas that are normally off-limits to individuals and you can then enjoy a journey unencumbered by the planning process.

If you're a first-time traveler, a group will help you dip your toes in the water of solo travel, while having a safety net to catch you if any issues arise.

Be aware, however, that single supplement fees are often tacked on to a tour for solo travelers. In essence, you're paying for two people. While I will admit to staying in places for as little as $2 a night, where single supplements are not an issue, hotels of any quality base their room rate on double occupancy, and don't give a discount if you're alone.

By booking early, some tour companies will guarantee that they will connect you with another solo traveler, or they will waive the single supplement completely. If the tour you choose won't waive the supplement, inquire if they can provide you with any additional perks, such as a free meal or drinks.

iExplore (www.iexplore.com) offers trips with a reduced single supplement charge, making the trip more affordable for those on their own. In addition, they offer private tours for solo travelers, giving you maximum flexibility on departure dates and itineraries.

Connecting: Solo Travel Network (www.cstn.org) links up travelers so that they can share experiences and costs (eliminating the single supplement fee for tours). While it may be risky to travel with someone you don't know, setting up clear expectations can make all the difference; and if it can save you hundreds of dollars, it may be well worth it.

Many tour companies operate trips solely for women that typically offer numerous activities and are geared for a wide range of comfort levels. Other companies offer tours that are primarily of interest to women. Bernice Notenboom, a contributing editor to *National Geographic Traveler*, owns Moki

Take a Tour

On a backpacker's budget while traveling through the Northern Territories of Australia, I found that joining a tour was the only way to enter Kakadu National Park. I bit the bullet and joined a tour group for a three-day trip.

My group was fortunate to have been appointed a tour guide with intimate knowledge of the area and a down-under sense of adventure. At one point, while careening down a dirt track in a four-wheel-drive vehicle, our guide suddenly pulled over to the side of the road and jumped out. Moments later, he returned from the bush with a frillynecked lizard in his hands. We all had the chance to hold this prickly beast. The memory of that lizard has stuck with me, and now I never quibble over the cost of joining a group with a knowledgeable guide.–BW

Treks (www.mokitreks.com). Her tour company offers culturally sensitive "vacations for the soul," with varying degrees of adventure tossed in. In her experience, "Women have a strong interest in native cultures," which is why the majority of her participants are female.

For more ideas on women-only tours, search the Internet or visit Wanderlust and Lipstick (www.wanderlustandlipstick. com) for tour information.

Elderhostels (www.elderhostel.org), a tour option for those 55 and over (not quite elders in my book), offers an excellent opportunity to travel with other like-minded people, while focusing on a distinct region or unique activity. Elderhostel is a not-for-profit organization that provides learning adventures from the exotic (such as a Mekong Delta tour in Southeast Asia) to the cultural (including Day of the Dead tours in

Mexico). These educational tours are generally all-inclusive, meaning everything but transportation to and from your destination is included in the cost.

Mildred, in her mid-80s, continues to travel every chance she gets, and has chosen Elderhostel for several journeys. "With Elderhostel, you can travel on your own, but you become part of a group. Not only are you seeing the sights, but you're attending programs and courses. They are always interesting, whether it's music or programs talking about nature. The food is good, healthful, and plentiful. These tours are definitely worthwhile."

⚘ Relaxation

Recharging and enjoying down time should be an integral part of life and travel. Whether you work 50 weeks of the year and need (and deserve) a couple of weeks of R&R or you would prefer a more active vacation that gets you away from your desk job, incorporating some beach or cabin time into all or part of your journey will help you feel rejuvenated when you return home.

Spas—If salt scrubs and daily yoga classes, horseback riding, or golf sound delightful to you, there are thousands of possibilities offered by spas and resorts located around the globe. Spa Finder (www.spafinder.com) offers a comprehensive listing of day, resort, and destination spas. Spa Finder's President, Susie Ellis, says, "Destination spas are perfect for solo women travelers because meals and activities happen as part of a group."

Book Your Own—For a low-budget option, create your own spa-like getaway by determining in what environment you feel most relaxed. Is it a beach? A lake cabin? A ski-in hut? Even on a small budget, you can make a reservation for a getaway at the accommodation of your choice and pack a yoga CD or DVD, some herbal tea bags, and a stack of books—and unplug. Each winter, I sneak off to a mountain cabin where I can cozy up to a fireplace with lots of reading material, with the knowledge that a masseuse and hot tub are nearby if I choose to use them, but they're not part of an expensive package.

A Short Splurge—For a break from your travels, you can choose to schedule a day at a beach. Or, if your budget allows, you can plan to splurge with a night's stay at an upscale accommodation with a luxurious pool facility. During a backpacking adventure through Southeast Asia, I took time out to relax at the pool of the prestigious Mandarin Oriental, in Bangkok.

✿ Pursue Your Hobby

If you spend your time at home engaging in a particular hobby, why not pursue it on the road? You may find that there are more opportunities to experience and participate in your favorite pastime at your destination than in your own backyard.

Photography—Many people travel solely to pursue their passion for photography. Not only will you come home with memories, but you'll be able to share the experience with others through slide shows (both off- and online), photo albums, and framed prints. I'm particularly fond of MyPublisher (www.mypublisher.com). This site allows you to upload photos and design your own photo album that MyPublisher then prints like a book. The user interface is simple, and shipping is fast. Online photo-sharing communities such as Flickr (www.flickr.com) allow you to share your digital treasures with the world, if you so choose.

2. TRAVEL IDEA GENERATOR

ᚠᚠᚠ Amy's Story ᚠᚠᚠ

I went to India for six months to learn about tea. In the beginning, I only had the email addresses of two or three people who knew someone who knew someone who might know something about tea. I decided one month after I got there that I would open a tea shop when I returned home to New Jersey. I spent the next five months there researching.

I met the head of a tea plantation in Guwahati, in the state of Assam, where there are more than 800 tea gardens. He introduced me to others, and I was invited to a wedding where I met even more people, who invited me to tour even more gardens. I think because I'm a woman, they all wanted to help me and were concerned about my traveling alone.

I felt like I received an international master's degree in six months for what would have been a two-year program.

Whether it's dance, culture, or clay pots, I encourage people to find something they enjoy to focus on. It really helped me to be traveling with a purpose, as opposed to just traveling to travel. This was especially helpful for me in India, where there are more than 600 languages, 30 states, every type of terrain, and every kind of food and fabric imaginable. It's all of life, all at once, and you can't take it in all at once. Having a focus made all the difference for me.

Look for additional photography suggestions in Chapter 10, Pack it Up, and Chapter 11, Gadgets and Gizmos.

Birdwatching—While I'm not a birdwatcher at home, I got hooked on birding during a trip to Costa Rica. All it took was a pair of binoculars and a pocketful of patience.

For a successful experience peppered with more than luck, hire a knowledgeable guide familiar with the area. In the Monteverde Cloud Forest, I sat for hours watching hummingbirds zip within inches of my head, attracted by multiple feeders in a small sanctuary. I even stumbled upon a toucan perched high above a tree outside my hotel room. However, for the pièce de résistance, it was a guide who pointed out a nesting (and quite rare), resplendent quetzal deep in the woods.

Organized birding tours are available worldwide, from New Jersey to Ethiopia.

Wildlife Viewing—Viewing and photographing animals in their natural habitats has become very popular the world over. It's relatively easy to see nesting eagles in British Columbia, Canada, and monarch butterflies in the oyamel fir forests of Mexico, as an independent traveler. Search on the Internet to find the wildlife your planned destination has to offer, or base your trip on where to observe your favorite wild animal. I once camped on the island of Assateague, (off the U.S.'s East Coast), to spend time among the wild horses for which the area is so famous. It was an easy trip to plan and get close to the wildlife.

This won't always be the case. Many of the world's best wildlife locations (think: African safari) will be remote and inaccessible, and are best (or only) experienced with a guide. I have joined tours that included nature guides and have attended free presentations from a park service. In all instances, my knowledge and the number of animals I viewed increased dramatically. A trained guide can pick out a camouflaged three-toed sloth hiding in the treetops, where my untrained eye only sees bark and leaves.

2. TRAVEL IDEA GENERATOR

Culinary Tourism—Food, glorious, food! Sampling regional foods (and drink) can bring you as close to a culture as any museum. And, as a woman traveling on her own, you may even have the incomparable experience of being invited into kitchens and homes to observe and help with the preparation of food.

Whether you simply appreciate interesting meals, are a whiz in the kitchen, or are serious about increasing your culinary skills, you can join the growing segment of travelers who plan their trips to experience the foods and wines of specific destinations. You don't have to be a connoisseur to enjoy gnocchi at a trattoria in Rome or satay skewers at a night market in Singapore. You only need a sense of adventure and the willingness to sample, sample, and then sample some more.

Cheryll, a cultural-exchange professional, has traveled to China eight times for business. On many occasions, she has found herself sitting in front of plates filled with duck head and tongues, cobra, and even a whole baby turtle. Since it's considered impolite to turn down food in China, especially when you have the seat of honor next to the host, she found a good way around not having to sample everything. "I've found that I don't have to eat the whole thing and that if I talk long enough, they'll eventually take the food away."

To get started on your culinary adventure, see the Dining Guides section in chapter 4, Mapping Out the Details.

For tasting and informational tours, book a trip with a company that will provide you with an insider's perspective on local foods through the personal experience of a guide. Such tours are available in places from New Orleans (www.noculinarytours.com) to South Africa (www.coastlinetravel.com), from Sonoma (www.beauwinetours.com) to Chile (www.crookedtrails.com).

To learn skills from an expert cook, sommelier or pastry chef, plan to spend a weekend or longer taking a hands-on workshop. You'll not only learn a new skill, but will be exposed to the local culture.

Volunteer—We should consider ourselves fortunate to have the financial means (and freedom) to travel the world. It's a luxury many people do not have. To give back to the community you'll be visiting can be extremely rewarding and will undoubtedly be appreciated by the locals.

Both not-for-profit organizations and for-profit companies offer volunteer opportunities for worthy projects around the world. Consider building housing for a disaster-ridden area, installing wells to ensure safe drinking water for a poor community in a developing country, or working as a health-care professional for a remote village clinic.

For organized volunteer programs, you pay to participate. However, it can be well worth it to be a steward of the Earth, to learn about other cultures and to dive into a project on your own with the safety net of being in an organized group.

Cross-Cultural Solutions (www.crossculturalsolutions.org) has nearly 200 volunteerism programs, from Ghana to Peru, which last between one and 12 weeks. Habitat for Humanity International (www.habitat.org), Global Volunteers (www. globalvolunteers.org), and Earthwatch Institute (www. earthwatch.org) are additional well-established organizations with volunteer programs.

Even if you don't have the time or finances to travel specifically to volunteer, you can build a volunteer experience into any trip. You don't need to be an expert to deliver clothes to an orphanage or to examine the status of a well-water project.

Tour Companies:

**To choose the one that's right for you,
ask the following questions:**

- Do they cover the destination where you want to travel?

- How long have they been in business?

- Are their prices comparable to other companies? Be suspect of tours priced at the low end—you get what you pay for, and they may skimp on the basics. Compare like programs between companies in terms of how many days their programs run and what amenities they offer.

- How experienced are their guides? Are they trained professionals or fresh out of college?

- What's the ratio between guides and paying customers?

- What age group and sex do they cater to and attract?

- What level of physical activity will the scheduled activities entail, and are you in good enough shape to participate?

- What can you expect from the daily schedule?

- Do they supply any special gear or equipment you might need?

- Will they provide you with references (past participants) whom you can contact by phone or email?

You only need to be a willing helper. One way to determine any special needs is to ascertain whether your home town has a sister-city organization where you'll be traveling. Visit the Sister Cities International website (www.sister-cities.org) to find out.

 Work and Travel

Many women choose to take a job in another area of their own country or in a completely different part of the world to add adventure and new experiences to their day-to-day routines. If you are fortunate enough to have a flexible employer, you could take an extended leave of absence and subsidize your travels with seasonal or temporary work. Some employers will provide opportunities (and even encourage you) to take a position within the company but in a different city or country for a designated period of time. If your employer doesn't offer these options, you could look for work in the place you'd like to visit, and then quit your job.

One summer, I drove to Alaska from New Jersey to work in a cannery. I had heard the money couldn't be beat. I was saving for a trip to Asia, and being able to experience Alaska while making what I anticipated would be a boatload of money was a bonus. A group of us were flown into remote Bristol Bay in a prop plane and stuck (and I do mean stuck) there for six weeks, processing salmon. The money was great because there was nothing to buy, nowhere to go, and nothing to do but work and eat free meals. While the conditions weren't ideal, flying over the snow-covered mountain ranges and exploring the tundra in this remote area were experiences I couldn't have afforded at the time on my backpacker's budget.

Because it doesn't require a long-term commitment, seasonal work is often a good choice for travelers. In North America, this type of temporary work can be found by searching for "seasonal" on sites such as Craigslist (www.craigslist.org). If you don't manage to line up something in advance, or you simply stumble upon an area where you'd like to spend additional time, you can check youth hostel message boards and temporary employment agencies for work opportunities.

2. TRAVEL IDEA GENERATOR

Erin bought a book on how to get work in the cruise industry, then spent months communicating with human resources departments. She eventually got a job on the *Queen Mary II*, and left behind her job and her home town. "I knew I wouldn't be able to travel without the financial support of a job, and being in a work environment made it easier because there was a structure. It was like one big family and, because we were all stuck on the ship, I got to know a lot of people."

✤ Learn about Other Cultures

For me, it's not a trip unless I can experience the local culture beyond scratching the surface. I may struggle with languages, yet I still have fun by visiting with residents and attending cultural events that help me get closer to the community.

Elyse Weiner, of the audio-tour company iJourneys, knows firsthand how travel and learning about cultures can affect your life. Her first trip was at age 19, backpacking for nine months around Europe, "Sending people out into the world opens their eyes and minds."

Jo "travels to the ends of the Earth" to pursue her passion for people. "The places I like best are the ones with intact cultures, ones that haven't been unduly influenced by Western ways of doing things."

Even if you don't plan to go to the ends of the Earth, treat yourself to an afternoon or evening of culture at your destination to increase your understanding of the local society and history. Time Out guides (www.timeout.com) offer entertainment and local information for many cities, from Abu Dhabi to Zurich. The city you're visiting may also have an English-language paper or magazine with event listings, or you can inquire at your hotel or tourist information center about current happenings.

Museums—From archeology to Native American art, museums offer insight into cultures both past and present. Start your visit to any city or town at a museum. Often the architecture of the building will reflect the region (such as the Louvre, in Paris) as much as the permanent collections inside.

Music, Dance, and Theater—You don't need to dig too deeply in order to experience traditional or typical music and dance from a region or country. Live music venues and performance halls will be listed online, in some guidebooks and in magazines created for visitors, such as the Time Out guides. Attend an event that suits your style (whether rock, jazz or traditional), and combine dinner out with a cultural experience!

On the island of Bali, the locals have made it easy to observe their traditions and still maintain their deeply held religious beliefs and practices, despite the throngs of tourists that visit every year. Since many of their ceremonies are private and cannot be attended by foreigners, instead, they present cultural evenings of dance and music as entertainment, while incorporating some of their spiritual beliefs. For less than 10 dollars, you can attend an outdoor event that includes fire walking or gamelan playing.

Festivals and Cultural Events—What better way to experience a culture than during a special occasion? There is a nearly infinite number of festivals that take place in locations around the world, many of them with unique offerings, such as the East Coast Blues and Roots Festival in Australia; the Boston International Comedy and Movie Festival; the Hoggetown Medieval Faire in Gainesville, Florida; or the Pushkar Camel Festival in Rajasthan, India.

While North America is their focus, Festivals.com (www. festivals.com) provides comprehensive listings of cultural events around the world.

You're sure to find a festival that suits a particular interest you have. The locale may be crowded and hotels will be in high demand, so it's essential to book early. Keep in mind, too, that event dates change from year to year.

✤ Genealogy

Ask any librarian, and he or she will tell you that genealogical research is on the rise. Traveling to study genealogy also happens to be ideal for the solo traveler. It gives you the freedom to move around and follow leads without being encumbered by a bored traveling partner. Researching your family history through visits to homes of distant relatives, libraries, genealogical centers, and cemeteries can give you purpose and direction during your travels. In addition, it's an easily "acceptable" form of travel for solo women. Who would dissuade you from traveling for such a noble purpose?

Of course, you're not limited to domestic travel. Most of us have family abroad. If your roots stretch overseas, devote a portion of your travel to tracking down a long-lost cousin. Carry a digital (or tape) recorder, camera and journal dedicated to your research so you can document the people you meet.

For online research prior to your trip, start with RootsWeb. com (www.rootsweb.com), which provides birth and death records for individuals, and connects people researching their family history. It only takes a few minutes to get hooked on this free site, as you search for information on relatives. RootsWeb's "parent," Ancestry.com (www.ancestry.com), provides more-sophisticated tools and access to additional information, for a membership fee.

❧❧❧ Ethel's Story ❧❧❧

I researched for my book about my ancestors for 11 years. I found that I had to prepare carefully before I traveled to a town, otherwise I could waste a lot of time.

I would find out if there was a genealogy room in the county library or a genealogical society that I could visit. I also checked with the local historical society and county courthouse for records. I learned to always call ahead or check online to find out their address and working hours. It was also good to know if I would have access to all their records. Sometimes they required 24 hours notice. Genealogy room volunteers can be most helpful. They are familiar with the local history and know the materials in their reading room. They live in the area and can give directions to courthouses, cemeteries or other archives.

I looked for the opportunity to meet "new" relatives in locations I visited. The ones I did meet varied in how interested they were in genealogy. Usually, they were willing to give me a few minutes. I let them know what I was doing and told them I would like to stop by to talk about the family tree. They were more willing to talk about their parents or grandparents than about their own families, at first. I approached them as a friendly visitor, and they opened up as they began to trust me. If they weren't interested at all, I asked them if someone else in the family might be, and then I had an introduction to a new family member who was more open to talking.

One of my best reasons for traveling is to meet kindred spirits whom I have met online or by mail. They are usually doing research on my family or one akin to it. I have many people across the country now whom I can contact for information, and several of them have offered me a place to stay. I live in Kentucky, and there is a woman in Port Angeles, Washington, who gave me an open invitation to her place!

GETTING BEYOND THE EXCUSES

TRAVELING *provides us with opportunities to see beyond the daily grind, as we experience the world in new ways. We all carry with us the expectation of what will be most difficult to overcome during a solo journey. Much of what we anticipate is nothing more than our own fears spinning tales of disaster in our heads, while other concerns are bona fide. With adequate preparation and tips from this chapter, you'll discover which ones are fantasy fears and how to overcome the others. And remember that while traveling solo can present numerous challenges, it also magnifies the richness of these experiences.*

✿ I would feel vulnerable

True, there is strength in numbers, and when traveling alone you may feel a bit disoriented, on top of feeling insecure, which has the potential to make you an easier target. It's difficult to be continuously alert, protecting yourself and your personal items, without having someone else around to pick up the slack. However, traveling with others may actually give you a false sense of security, as you tend to let down your guard more easily when others are around.

If you put thought into where and when to travel, practice good safety measures, and follow the suggestions and tips throughout this book, you'll be prepared to have a safe and joyous journey and the experience of a lifetime, with memories that you can share with friends for years to come.

✿ I'm in a relationship and/or have children

If you are in a committed relationship, married, or have kids, you may believe that it's impossible to take a solo vacation. It's true that it may be difficult due to logistical issues (needing a babysitter and keeping up with your bills), and you may receive some resistance from your family. However, there are many women who are in just these types of situations who are able to find the time and resources, and receive the understanding from their families to take a journey by themselves. Particularly if you have children, it could be just the mental-health break you've needed.

As part of a couple or a family, we can become accustomed to relying on others to plan, to make decisions, and to handle small and large details in our lives. The result is that we can lose sight of who we are.

As you'll discover throughout this book, traveling on your own can make you a stronger person. In turn, that can help strengthen the bonds in your significant relationships. An understanding partner will be supportive of your decision to get away to follow a dream that he or she may not share. You may want to start with a short trip, to begin with. Regardless of how long you can go for, do go! You owe it to yourself.

❧ I don't feel comfortable eating alone

Being self-conscious about eating alone in a restaurant is probably one of the reasons fast-food joints and drive-throughs are so prolific. Dining alone is an uncomfortable experience for most of us. But that's only because we aren't accustomed to it.

So, how do you get around the awkwardness of dining by yourself? First, accept the fact that not everyone is staring at you.

Second, keep yourself preoccupied. Bring a book, magazine, newspaper, or your travel journal. There's nothing worse than staring into space at a restaurant without anything to focus on. Sit in the bar of a restaurant, where it better accommodates solo diners. Chat with the bartender, watch TV, or grab the local real estate listings or newspaper.

To practice dining on your own, start small: Pay a visit to a local coffee shop, grabbing a hot drink and reading the paper. Or, head 20 miles outside of town and find an interesting diner or café where you can treat yourself to lunch. Solo. Or find a hidden gem of a restaurant in your town where you can relax and eat at your own pace. Whatever you choose, enjoy the chance to savor a meal on your own.

Marya Charles Alexander, editor and publisher of SoloDining. com (www.solodining.com), suggests that women make a reservation for dining out. "It will discern you from others and will give you the opportunity to determine whether they value solo diners. Ask what time they have the most solo diners, where they seat them, and whether they comp any menu items for those on their own. Making a reservation is empowering!"

❦ Being alone is lonely

A misconception of traveling solo is that you'll be lonely. While traveling on your own can get lonely at times, the reality is . . . and you have to trust me on this . . . traveling is one of the most social of activities because you'll meet lots of people on the road, some of whom you'll engage in fleeting conversations (perhaps at the train station or in the lobby of a pension), and some whom will become friends for life who visit you annually. Regardless of where you go, you will meet them.

I spent my 30th birthday in the outback of Australia, in the country's center. I rose at 4:30 a.m., along with about 50 other campers, to watch the sun come up behind Uluru (the grand monolith also known as Ayers Rock). My traveling companions, with whom I'd hitched a ride just days prior, treated me to a happy birthday postcard and cupcake, candle and all. What could have been a sad and forlorn experience was made memorable by a small gesture from new friends.

You'll only be alone if you want to be. And when that twinge of loneliness does hit, there are many things you can do to help stave it off (see Chapter 14, Getting Acquainted).

❦ I'll get bored

When you're traveling, every day brings new opportunities and interesting options. You'll look at the world with new eyes, seeing things you couldn't have dreamed about, and be bombarded with sights, sounds, and smells you couldn't have imagined. You'll find yourself in a naturally elevated state of euphoria from being exposed to new cities, villages, and surrounded by new sensations.

Most often, you'll have difficulty squeezing in everything. Laura explains, "For everything you do on a trip, there are an infinite number of things you don't do." You can always make a return trip!

I'm shy

Many of us feel that we're too shy to travel without having someone else to rely on. We may even insulate ourselves in our homes and at work, and can't imagine conversations with strangers. While traveling, however, you'll find that you're more likely to come out of your shell because no one knows you and you have nothing to lose.

You can even practice traveling on your own simply by driving to a small town near your home where you will be anonymous. Have lunch or go to an afternoon movie. Make it a point to meet and talk with others. You'll see how easy it really is.

I'm too old

Fair enough. Your body is older and you may be a little slower than you used to be. That shouldn't stop you, however. Meg Noble Peterson, author of *Madam, Have You Ever Really Been Happy? An Intimate Journey Through Africa and Asia*, climbed Mt. Kilimanjaro to celebrate her 80th birthday. She suggests, "Don't let anyone push you too fast. Go at your own speed, and take plenty of time and make plenty of stops," especially when climbing at high altitudes!

It's a good idea to schedule down time to relax, and be sure not to overdo the number of activities you'd like to pursue. Get your insurance and medications in order, and pack lightly so that you don't have to carry around heavy luggage.

Marion travels regularly for her business and believes traveling is what helps her stay young at heart. At 80, she doesn't appear to be slowing down. "It's a wonderful experience, to keep traveling and to see new things. It's a large part of what's keeping me young."

In some respects, Beverly, who can be found traveling the world on her bicycle, finds traveling easier as she gets older. She says, "You get a lot less hassle from the guys. You have more confidence and can look guys in the eyes. You're less eager to please, and you get into less trouble."

❀ I wouldn't know where to go

If you don't already have some ideas for a dream journey, all you really need is a bit of imagination and a couple of travel magazines, such as *National Geographic Adventure* (www.adventure. nationalgeographic.com) or *Arthur Frommer's Budget Travel* (www.budgettravelonline.com) to find inspiration. There are excellent independent bookstores around the country specializing in travel, which can provide you with individualized attention. Libraries and travel-based websites are additional resources for inspiration and ideas.

If you can dream it, you can do it. Don't underestimate the power of your imagination and your ability to make things materialize.

Start with the Dream Trip Worksheet on page 36, and then start setting aside your cash to make it happen.

✻ I can't take time off from work

While most of us are at the mercy of an employer, every job allows for at least some time off, whether it's a long weekend or an extended vacation planned a year out. Accumulate your vacation time and personal days, and make plans to use them. According to a study conducted by Harris Interactive for Expedia, the typical European's vacation time ranges from 20 to 40 days, while Americans typically earn 12 and Canadians 21 days of vacation each year. We Americans are sorely deprived in terms of vacation time, so we should not feel intimidated about taking the time we have earned.

Use it, don't lose it! It took Andrea, an advertising executive in New York City, many years with the same company to take her much-needed vacation time. "Years ago, I felt like I couldn't take time off. I now realize that I work my butt off and, after so many years of losing vacation, there's no way I won't take the time now. Vacation time is so precious. It's a mental health break more than anything, and helps you get your life in order. You need to get away from the office."

Some employers allow for a long-term leave of absence while guaranteeing the same position when the employee returns. It's unpaid, of course, but an opportunity nonetheless, to travel for an extended period if you make arrangements ahead of time. As a lawyer working for her state's government, Elizabeth planned well in advance for her three months of leave to go to Africa. "I presented my trip to the company nearly two years prior to going. By the time it came around, it had all been signed off and OK'd. I came back to 800 emails and everything was the same!"

Depending on your work environment and situation, you may be able to explain the importance of travel in your life to

Dream Trip Worksheet

The top four places I'd like to go if cost were not an issue are:

1. _____

2. _____

3. _____

4. _____

Estimate the costs:

Dream Trip 1:   **Dream Trip 2:**

Airfare _____   Airfare _____

Hotels _____   Hotels _____

Food _____   Food _____

Local   Local
Transportation _____   Transportation _____

Entertainment _____   Entertainment _____

Souvenirs _____   Souvenirs _____

Other _____   Other _____

Dream Trip 3:

Airfare _____

Hotels _____

Food _____

Local
Transportation _____

Entertainment _____

Souvenirs _____

Other _____

Dream Trip 4:

Airfare _____

Hotels _____

Food _____

Local
Transportation _____

Entertainment _____

Souvenirs _____

Other _____

Five creative ways I can save or make money to pay for my
Dream Trip(s):

1. _____

2. _____

3. _____

4. _____

5. _____

your employer and then work on mutually agreeable terms in which your work is covered during your hiatus. Beverly set the boundaries with her job and made it clear that she would quit if she didn't get the time off that she felt she needed. "I live my life such that I can travel."

I have an illness or disability

Having an illness or disability doesn't need to be a showstopper for your wanderlust. And while traveling with special needs may not be easy, it is easier now than it has ever been.

Nancy Berger, author of *Disabled Travelers Guide to the World* (www.disabledtravelersguide.com), is a true inspiration. She has been disabled for 20 years, yet she hasn't allowed her wheelchair to slow her down. She has visited all seven continents. "There are many wonderful experiences and discoveries you truly should not miss. Life is too short to skip them, and being disabled is no reason why you shouldn't go. I know this from experience."

Let the proprietors of your hotel, bed and breakfast, or campground know what your circumstances are, and ask them to keep an eye on you. This is a tip for all solo women, but it should particularly be followed for those who have special needs. Carry a whistle to alert others if you need help. Chapter 9, Staying Healthy on the Road, offers additional tips.

There are a wide variety of tours available these days for people with special needs. Among them are: Accessible Journeys (www.disabilitytravel.com), which arranges group and individual tours for people in wheelchairs. Access-Able Travel Source (www.access-able.com), which features information on accommodations, attractions, transportation, and equipment rental for disabled travelers. And DisabledTravelers.com (www.disabledtravelers.com), which provides a comprehensive listing of tour operators, accessible cruise operators, adventure travel guides, and home exchanges.

Jo contracted a bone-eating bacteria on her way to Timbuktu, in Mali, which left her disabled. Since that accident (see her story in Chapter 9, Staying Healthy on the Road), she admits that she's had to change some things about her travel. "Up until my accident a few years ago, I traveled by public transportation. In third-world countries I now take taxis because even a wheeled bag is too difficult and risky to carry around. And I now use porters because I can't take a bag down stairs." However, these obstacles haven't stopped her from continued travel.

Take advantage of the resources and information now available to help plan your next (or first) adventure. Focus on what's possible, rather than what might get in your way.

🜏 What if I get lost?

I once drove for two hours in the wrong direction before I realized that I wasn't supposed to smell the salty sea air heading west from New Jersey. We've all driven past our turnoff on the highway, missed a train stop, or become utterly confused in a city and had to ask for help.

It's almost inevitable that you'll get lost. If you don't, you're not being adventurous! There are, however, ways to prevent going too far astray, such as carrying maps, a cell phone or calling card, the business card of your hotel written in the local language, and a list of emergency contacts. If you're driving in North America, it's a good idea to have a roadside-assistance membership with the American Automobile Association (www.aaa.com) or the Canadian Automobile Association (www.caa.ca).

❧ What if I get sick?

I know many women who are uncomfortable with the idea of traveling because of the germ factor. They want to avoid getting sick and don't want to be in constant contact with what they perceive to be unsanitary conditions.

While it's true that you may be exposed to more germs while traveling, if you follow standard health protocols, the odds are good you won't fall ill.

Whether it starts out as something simple, like Delhi Belly, or something more complicated, like dengue fever, you'll want to get help from a professional if you believe your illness is serious. Pay close attention to the progress of your symptoms, and see a doctor if they don't improve in a couple of days. Your country's embassy can guide you as to where expatriates go for medical assistance.

With proper precautions, such as getting vaccinations, using mosquito repellent, following safe eating and drinking habits, and staying alert for hazards specific to the area you're visiting, you will be able to successfully avoid most health problems. And if you still get sick, there are plenty of options and people willing to help when you're traveling solo.

❧ I only speak English

While travel is more fun and interesting when you can communicate with the locals, you don't need to master another tongue to enjoy yourself. It's polite to learn at least a few words and phrases before arrival, but English is spoken in most major cities, and you can always rely on a phrasebook or dictionary.

If you can say in the local language, "How do you say . . ." and then point to an object, you will immediately break down

Meeting Locals

While sitting on a park bench at the zocalo (central square) in Oaxaca, Mexico, I was enjoying the peaceful setting and studying my phrasebook, attempting to learn a few more words of Spanish. A young man noticed my intense studying and approached me to practice his English. For words I didn't understand, I pointed to objects, looked them up in my book, and then got coaching from my new teacher. A lively "conversation" ensued as we shared our languages through words, phrases, and hand gestures.

We parted ways without my having a much deeper understanding of the language, but with a cross-cultural exchange that remains etched in my memory.—BW

communication barriers. People will respect your willingness to try and you may even make a friend.

Read Chapter 16, Hurdling Language Barriers, for more specific information.

✿ What will other people think?

Peer pressure is no small part of why some women won't travel. Your loved ones may not understand how you could take a trip, leaving behind family, friends, and perhaps your significant other and children.

When Supriya was 31, she quit her job to travel throughout Asia and Europe before entering Wharton Business School for her MBA. When she told her friends about her plans of quitting her job and traveling, they tried to dissuade her. "I believe they were threatened by the change and how it would affect them. It broke the inertia of their own lives."

For support, align yourself with other women you know who have traveled. Read travel books and stories by women, and be confident in the fact that you're not alone in your desire to travel on your own.

Next time someone shares with you a plan that's outside of the box, congratulate them and wish them well.

The locals will be even harder to convince that what you're doing is "normal." Beverly says, "The culture gap is so huge to explain why I'm really traveling on my own. Instead of explaining, I invented a husband who died, as well as children who had their own children. This explained why I wasn't married and why my own children weren't with me. They had to stay home with their own kids."

✤ I don't think I can afford to travel

Not having enough dough can put a damper on a lot of things. But I promise that if you make travel a priority in your life, the rewards will be priceless. I don't recommend going into debt to fund your trip, but you can make plans to travel on a budget and, with some discipline, save for a low-cost trip that will give you stories to tell for years to come.

To fund my trips when I was younger, I would work three jobs and save all of my money until I had enough to take a couple months off. I worked for a temp agency doing office work during the day, I delivered pizza at night, and worked at a radio station on the weekends. None of them paid very much (which is why I had to have three jobs), but I wouldn't have had it any other way. I worked my butt off, and then happily quit them all and drove to Alaska from New Jersey.

I'm not suggesting you work three jobs to afford travel. There are lots of less-painful ways to accomplish the same aim.

Saving money can be as simple as a number of smaller measures, such as bringing your lunch to work and tucking away that extra $30 a week that you're currently spending on meals, or selling spare books and CDs that are collecting dust on your bookshelf on Amazon.com (www.amazon.com) or Craigslist (www.craigslist.org). Put that "extra" money away for your travel fund.

If you really want to travel, you'll learn to redirect your priorities (see Chapter 12, Legal Tender). Before you know it, you'll have saved for a weekend away, a week at the beach in Puerto Vallarta, or three weeks in Peru!

Getting Started

- When you're home alone, keep the radio and TV off. This will get you used to being in your own head, enjoying your own company.

- Leave work and have lunch by yourself, tomorrow.

- Leave the grrrrlfriends at home and go shopping by yourself. Take a half day in the afternoon (when the malls are quiet) and window shop.

- Go to the library and spend an hour examining travel books and magazines.

- Try starting light conversations with someone you would never normally talk to—a bus driver, the cashier at the grocery store, the person next to you on the Stairmaster at the gym. Anyone.

- Next time you have a free evening alone, treat yourself to a poetry reading, a foreign movie, or a new restaurant. Try something completely different in which your friends or family may not be interested. Your local newspaper or Citysearch (www.citysearch.com) will be loaded with ideas.

- Next time you travel with someone, schedule some time on your own. Go for a hike, take a walk on the beach, grab a meal by yourself, or have a coffee and read the latest copy of *National Geographic Traveler*.

- Does your husband or significant other work long hours and weekends? Take advantage of a busy time in his/her life by making time for yourself. Go for a long scenic drive in the country. Hike a trail you've only read about.

- Take an overnight trip to someplace close to home. Camp, stay in a youth hostel, or luxuriate at an upscale spa or resort. You'll feel like you've conquered the world!

- Invite yourself to visit a friend who lives in another city or state. Make it an overnight trip or a weekend in which your friends, family, or significant other stays home. This will help get you used to making the journey by yourself, and that's a big step.

Get out of your comfort zone. This is what travel's all about. You're going to be thrust into completely new situations, cultures, environments, currencies, languages, foods, beds, habits, schedules, adventures, transportation modes, and circumstances. That's the beauty of travel. Who wants McDonald's and Marriotts when you can choose small cafés and family-run pensions? You'll be challenged—embrace it!

4

MAPPING OUT THE DETAILS

WITH *a dream trip in mind, now you need to acquire the information necessary to make the trip happen. In this initial planning stage, there are numerous factors that will help you determine where and when to travel. With thorough research, which you'll learn how to do here, you can narrow down the many locations and types of travel to put together a trip that suits your needs perfectly.*

✤ Planning

Answering the following four questions will be a great start in determining where your next adventure may take you.

✤ What interests you?

As discussed in Chapter 2, Travel Idea Generator, there are many reasons for and ways to travel. What is it that impassions you and will get your motor running toward the destination you've dreamed about? Is it a hobby? Your need for down time? Or your fascination with a particular culture?

Don't discount the possibilities because nothing is beyond your reach. When you've narrowed down your goals and travel options, things will all fall into place.

I have a running mental list of what areas I'd like to visit next. Currently, this includes the Amazon rainforest and Papua New Guinea. Once the travel dream is at the forefront of my mind, I begin to collect magazine articles, travel stories and pertinent books. I keep a folder of where-to-go options and, as the time gets closer to deciding, all of my information is at the tip of my fingers.

✤ Where is it easiest to travel?

Every woman will have her own interpretation of what she considers to be an "easy" place to travel. One woman may feel completely at home in Bangladesh, while others may feel as if they've landed on another planet.

Regardless of whether your travels will take you somewhere in your own country or abroad, you can ease yourself into the travel experience by starting with places that have some familiarity for you. Venture out to cities where you have friends

Know Where You're Going

- Do the people at your destination speak English?

- Is the transportation system reliable?

- Is the government stable?

- What sort of government is in control (capitalist, dictatorship, socialist, etc.)?

- Are the men known for their macho behavior?

- Are the country's traditions prejudicial against women?

- Are the women residents oppressed?

- Is there a specific dress code for women?

- Is the region known for violence?

- Is the country currently involved in a civil war?

or connections. Or, begin with a country where people speak your native language or one in which you are well versed.

Every woman will also have a different tolerance level for what she considers a challenge. Audrey, a wife and mother of three from Connecticut, has traveled internationally for business and pleasure. She's a tough cookie and, having grown up in New Jersey, is probably a bit more street savvy than most. "I've never felt threatened, but I've always been smart about not getting myself into a position that was dangerous." She stays vigilant and observant.

For up-to-date alerts issued by the U.S. government, check the U.S. Department of State's website (www.travel.state.gov). Here, you'll find recommendations on which countries Americans are urged to avoid, whether because of civil unrest or other factors. The CIA's (yes, *that* CIA) World Factbook (www.cia.gov/cia/publications/factbook) is packed with information about every country, and includes statistics on population, geography, land size, and much more.

If you really want to travel to a particular country that might be questionable for Western women to visit, then act and dress accordingly, ignore cat calls, wear sunglasses to avoid eye contact, and GO! I would never discourage someone from traveling to their dream destination.

What's the length of your trip?

The amount of time you have to travel will help you narrow down where you can physically go. Determine how many days, weeks, or months your schedule and finances will allow, and maximize both by budgeting (see Chapter 12, Legal Tender). You'll never regret using the greatest amount of time possible to travel.

If you have just one week, you probably won't want to commit to a trip in which the flight will take a full day (Los Angeles to Delhi, for instance), but you can plan a vacation closer to home (Los Angeles to Hawaii or Mexico). Save the long flights for a time frame when you can actually get over jet lag!

If you do have three months to travel, but dollars are tight, rent out your home, participate in a house swap, or work along the way. If you have a couple of weeks with some cash to spend, treat yourself to nicer accommodations or schedule a few tours or day trips to maximize sightseeing.

When can you travel?

Timing may not be everything, but it can be important. When I had more free time to travel, I didn't care as much about when or where I was going. I just wanted to go. Now that my vacation time is more limited, I want to make sure that my adventures include the best weather and the smallest crowds.

Travel is cheapest during the shoulder seasons when tourists haven't started flocking to a destination or have all returned home following summer. During shoulder seasons, airfare and hotel prices will be lower, restaurants and tourist attractions will be less crowded, and the weather still quite pleasant.

Be aware that shops, restaurants, and hotels in some countries close down during what you would think might be the height of tourism. Europe is notorious for its businesses closing during August because the locals are traveling elsewhere. Hotels will be open in Mexico during Semana Santa, but many stores and restaurants will close in the weeks building up to this Easter holiday week. You can bet that when schools are on holiday, families will be, too. Adjusting your plans by just one week can make a big difference in encountering fewer people.

Guidebooks will not only list the best times to visit with regards to weather, but they may also include festivals and events, and what to expect during each month. Earth Calendar (www.earthcalendar.net) is a fun website on which you can view dates for holidays around the world.

❧ Guidebooks

There are a handful of really stellar guidebooks that cover a breadth of locations in great depth. I'm a passionate guidebook gal and, unfortunately, there's not enough room here to extol the virtues of them all, so I'll provide info on my faves and then list some additional publishers. It really is a personal preference, however, and the best guidebook for your destination might not even be from one of the publishers below.

The Lonely Planet (www.lonelyplanet.com) guides are the most entertaining and comprehensive. With more than 600 titles available, they also publish phrasebooks, maps, and coffee-table photo books. Initially, Lonely Planet appealed to the backpacker set, but their award-winning books grew to include mid- to higher-end accommodations and dining, and they are now the definitive guides to most everywhere, for everyone. I start every trip with Lonely Planet.

Rough Guides (www.roughguides.com) have moved close to the top for me. They are an excellent alternative (or addition) to Lonely Planet, and include more than 75 countries and nearly 100 cities.

Dorling Kindersley (www.dk.com) travel guides are chock full of photos, and provide a snapshot peek at the world. These are excellent go-to guides to get a sense of place and to help you plan your sightseeing.

Other top-rated publishers include Moon Handbooks, Fodor's, Frommer's, Insiders' Guide, Bradt Travel Guides, Footprint Travel Guides, and Time Out.

Buy the most recent edition of a guidebook. Even the latest guide can be two years old. The longer the recommendation has been in print, the more likely rates will have increased and the hotspots will be well worn or, worse yet, out of business.

In the same way you might avoid movie reviews because they can cloud how you view a movie, Coleen cautions to not take your guidebook too seriously. "A lot of things you read in books color your experience. I don't let what I read contaminate what I see." In other words, appreciate these guides for the information they can provide, but don't rely on them 100 percent.

☙ Travel Magazines

Monthly travel magazines are filled with inspirational stories, tips, in-depth destination-specific articles, photographs, and general information. Try *Condé Nast Traveler*, *Arthur Frommer's Budget Travel*, *Outside*, *National Geographic Traveler*, *National Geographic Adventurer*, *Travel + Leisure*, *travelgirl* and the many others you can find at your favorite newsstand. (These all have an online presence, as well.) Personally, I subscribe to most of these (apologies to the mail carrier) and glean information from every issue.

☙ Forums

You've probably read some guidebooks that have provided you with an overview in terms of where to stay and what sights to visit. But did your guidebook tell you there's an excellent vegetarian restaurant in the Montmartre section of Paris called Rayons de Sante? Did you know that there's a gelato store, Amormo, near the Buci market with handmade gelati and a line of eager patrons that often runs down the street? And did you know that men on the Metro have a habit of rubbing themselves against single women travelers?

I found all these tidbits on various online forums. Forums are usually found within an already-established site and are where up-to-the-minute information is shared. You can post your experiences and recommendations and ask questions for others to answer.

☙ Blogs

Travel blogs have become a valuable and ever-expanding resource for information that may include anything from destination-specific to general tips. While many people write blogs to document their journeys for family and friends, the more

Informative Forums

Prior to a recent trip to Costa Rica, I monitored forums for suggested places to stay. Since I was traveling during Semana Santa (Holy Week), which happens to be when all of Central America goes on vacation, it was very difficult to find available hotels. However, with information acquired in forums, I was able to find some of the most offbeat places to visit, find out the latest scams used against tourists, and book accommodations.

One such accommodation was an eco-friendly beach hotel located 30 minutes from a dirt strip that functioned as the Osa Peninsula's airport. The hotel was run by a courageous woman who'd sold all of her belongings in Germany to take over day-to-day management of the business. While it lacked electricity and running water during the day, it more than made up for its lack of luxury through its charm and excellent breakfasts and dinners (which were shared, family-style, by all guests). Being right on the beach was a bonus.–BW

popular ones are updated regularly, over a long period of time. They often include personalized reviews, opinions, and information. Reading several blogs on a given topic will invariably provide you with wisdom of the crowds.

Technorati (www.technorati.com) tracks millions of blogs, and offers a search feature that can help you find information on even the most obscure subjects. Check out Wanderlust and Lipstick, where numerous women blog about various aspects of travel. Or, simply search for blogs on Google (www.blogsearch.google.com).

Dining Guides

Whether you're a foodie or not, you can maximize your travel experience by learning about the local cuisine and discovering food recommendations from those who know the area. If you're traveling within the United States, check out *Roadfood* (www. roadfood.com), by Jane and Michael Stern, for the best in casual eateries. Their book and website lists everything from bakeries to cafés to roadhouse stands to taco-mobiles. Citysearch provides restaurant listings in major cities throughout the United States. And the online forum Chowhound (www.chowhound. com) can help you find personalized recommendations for restaurants around the world. Take a moment and have fun with this one for your hometown or your travels!

Zagat Survey (www.zagat.com) provides the most comprehensive restaurant guides available. Accessible in both print and online formats, they use a customer survey approach, and include hotels, nightspots, and attractions. Zagat covers 95 countries worldwide and now provides a downloadable version for your phone.

For European travel, Michelin Guides (www.viamichelin.com) provide restaurant listings for cities in 42 countries. Don't let the one-star rating of a restaurant fool you. Michelin's prestigious system is quite stingy with their stars, and you'll be lucky to find a three-star (their highest-rated) restaurant where you're going.

The Eat Smart Guides (www.eatsmartguides.com) cover about 10 popular destinations, from Indonesia to Poland. Each book includes recipes, historical culinary information, and a list of menu items common to the country. The level of detail included in their books make the authors' passion for food and travel palpable.

If you're traveling with a guidebook, it's likely that a wide range of restaurant suggestions will be listed, from café-style bistros to high-end reservation-only gastronomical delights.

Additional resources for dining options include tourism offices, free city guides, and message boards at train stations and other public facilities.

🌀 Maps

Road maps. Laminated street maps. Printed pages from your guidebook. Printed pages from the web. Downloaded maps to your cell phone. So many maps, so little time.

When it comes to maps, I personally stick to low tech and lightweight. I photocopy pages from my guidebook and carry them around with me as I walk a city, or buy a small, foldable street map from a local shop. If you prefer something a bit more high tech, try downloading maps from an online resource such as Mapquest Mobile (www.mapquest. com/mobile), or Google (www.maps.google.com) to your cell phone.

Simone Andrus, owner of Wide World Books & Maps (www.wideworldtravels.com) in Seattle, knows how important a map can be to having a successful trip. "There are no bad maps, just mismatched maps for your purpose. For your initial planning stages, you'll want a small-scale map that covers a larger area. When you get down to figuring out what you want to do, you'll want a larger-scale version with street-level detail. Many guidebooks now come with maps on the inside cover."

Like guidebooks, most maps are updated every two or three years. While they won't change much between printings, you'll want to get the most recent version.

Simone adds, "The majority of my customers are women, as they are the ones doing the planning and asking for help."

5.

LET'S GET BOOKING

I LOVE *booking airline tickets. It's the first key to unlocking travel plans, and for me it's like cracking open a new book. Making my travel arrangements is filled with promise and the anticipation of adventure. I understand, however, that it can be a daunting task for some, particularly for those not well versed in all things Internet, since so much of making arrangements is done on the web today. This chapter will provide well-tested insider tips for successfully getting your plans in order—hassle-free.*

❦ When to Book

Whether traveling domestically or internationally, in most countries, it makes economical sense to book your flights in advance. Even the day before is preferable to booking the day of your flight at the airport. Some airlines will offer fixed pricing on flights regardless of when you travel or when you make your reservation, and will provide one-way tickets that are half the roundtrip cost. Most airlines, however, charge based on availability, the need to fill their flights, and the going rate at competitive airlines, causing a fluctuation in the cost.

As soon as you know where and when you're going, buy your tickets. If you have some flexibility in your schedule, booking engines can scan a range of dates to locate the best deal.

If you're traveling from the United States, last-minute tickets are usually outrageously expensive unless you purchase through a discount last-minute online resource, such as Lastminute.com (www.lastminute.com), or you have a travel agent who can find a deal for you.

❦ Major Search Engines

Buying tickets directly with an airline can sometimes be cheaper than reserving through one of the travel search engines. You'll also get better customer service if an issue arises than if you booked through a third party.

Having said that, I do start my search for flights, hotels, and car rentals on Expedia (www.expedia.com), Orbitz (www.orbitz.com), and Travelocity (www.travelocity.com). These sites sort flight information for most, but not all, airlines, hotels, and car-rental agencies. Pricing can be different between these search engines, depending on route, dates, destination, and travel times. Additional fees, such as fuel surcharges, booking fees, and taxes, may not be added until you're ready to check out, so read the fine print. Be aware that the airline may also charge fees based on the amount of luggage you are checking.

I confirm whether I'm being quoted a one-way or a round trip, and once I have found the cheapest price on one of these sites, I then call the airline, hotel, or car-rental agency directly or look at their website to find their best deal. Often it's the same or slightly better. If so, I book it.

You can also arrange multi-destination journeys on many of these sites. This option can be used if you are flying into one city and out of another, or if you are traveling to multiple locations and don't want to book one-way fares. You may also be able to search for flexible dates. In this case, the booking engine will search for several days surrounding your travel dates for the best deal.

Regional and smaller airlines such as Southwest Airlines (www.southwest.com) and JetBlue Airways (www.jetblue.com) aren't included on the major search engines, so you'll need to check their sites separately.

Hot Tip! On any website for which you use a credit card, you will see a lock icon at the bottom of your browser, which indicates that it's secure to enter your confidential information. If it doesn't appear, don't enter your credit card number.

If you've booked your flight and later find an identical flight on the same airline for less, some airlines will refund all or a portion of the difference in cost. Fares can go up or down several times in a day. Get to know what your airline's policy is, and then look periodically to see if the fare has been lowered. JetBlue, for instance, will credit you the difference if the fare for your flight has gone on sale after you've booked. If you book online, Northwest Airlines (www.nwa.com) will refund you the difference and give you a credit voucher worth $50 for future travel if you find a fare more than $5 cheaper than the original fare.

Farecast (www.farecast.com) is designed to forecast the rise and fall of pricing on flights using complicated algorithms and trends. By checking this site, you can determine the chance of it costing you less if you wait a couple of days before booking your flight.

Schedule flights early in the day, as these will be less prone to delay. The Bureau of Transportation Statistics (www.bts.gov) provides an amazing array of information on their website, including data for on-time performance of airlines, broken down by originating airports.

It's often cheaper and more convenient (there's less air and road traffic) to fly into a smaller airport, rather than a city's larger and more popular facility. On a business trip to Washington, D.C., I flew into Baltimore/Washington International Airport, rather than Dulles International. I saved nearly $100, and was able to fly on an airline that accepted my frequent-flier miles. I got upgraded to first class, too!

Beyond the Major Search Engines

Meta-search engines scan data from hundreds of travel sites, consolidate it, and then provide you with the lowest prices available. You don't book directly on these sites, but instead, they will direct you to the websites with the best deals. Two such sites are Kayak (www.kayak.com) and SideStep (www.sidestep.com). My experience is that sometimes the price increases between the initial one quoted and when I actually book. You'll want to pay close attention to the cost.

Lastminute.com is a reliable booking engine for last-minute weekend getaways. This site offers reduced airfare that includes either hotel accommodations or a car rental. Even if you don't need these add-ons, the package is usually less than just the airfare if purchased elsewhere. Times and flights are limited, and you can't book more than two weekends out.

WhichBudget (www.whichbudget.com) offers flight listings of low-cost carriers around the globe. Originally started in Europe to accommodate travelers who were country-hopping on these carriers for weekend trips, it now includes information on hundreds of airports and thousands of flying routes.

❀ E-tickets vs. Paper Tickets

In the majority of cases, you will receive an e-ticket when making an online plane reservation. An e-ticket is nothing more than a confirmation for your flights. The greatest benefit of the e-ticket system is that you'll never have to worry about losing your ticket because your reservation is linked through a central reservation system. You can literally arrive at the airport with just your ID and luggage.

On occasion, you may be given a paper ticket by default (and charged an additional fee for it) or given the option to receive a paper ticket (though I can't think of a good reason why you'd want one).

The International Air Transport Association (www.iata.org) is taking the lead role in implementing an e-ticket-only system. A spokesperson there cautioned, however, that "some developing countries won't have the technology to implement the e-ticket program." Ideally, this will be adopted worldwide in the near future.

❧ Reward Programs

Many airlines, car-rental agencies, hotel chains and credit-card companies offer point-accumulation programs that reward you for loyalty to one company. You can often receive mileage for staying at hotels or renting a car, or build up your rewards for free rentals or hotel stays. You don't have to fly, rent, or stay often for the rewards to add up. Loyalty matters over frequency.

I often get upgraded to first class on Northwest as a result of my loyalty in their mileage program. I'm even willing to pay a bit more for tickets (which is exactly what they rely on) to fly with Northwest or a partner carrier.

If there's a city to which you often travel for business or pleasure, determine which hotels and car-rental companies there offer programs with the fastest path to rewards.

To book flights using your frequent-flier miles, call the airline directly for the best service. Airlines are increasingly cutting back on the number of seats they make available to those using frequent-flier miles, so be flexible on your travel dates. Check back often if nothing is immediately available, as seats open up on occasion when customers cancel their reservations. (When you utilize frequent-flier miles, airlines allow you to hold a seat and then cancel it within a given number of days without losing your mileage.)

Most established major airlines allow you to purchase seats 330 days in advance of departure (using currency or frequent-flier awards). Advance ticketing schedules vary with smaller, newer airlines, however, and it is up to their discretion as to when they will release seats for award reservations. I discovered this when attempting to book a flight to India. I called often, starting one year out, until I was finally able to find seats that had opened up.

While I have booked flights using my frequent-flier miles, I prefer using them for upgrades since traveling during the shoulder season is relatively inexpensive. Why use my mileage when I can get cheap tickets? I purchased tickets to Costa Rica for less than $400 and then upgraded to first class using my miles—what a way to start a vacation! Note that it is difficult (though not impossible) to find seating availability during peak travel times using frequent-flier miles.

Travel Brokers

Travel Agents—While they may not be your cheapest option, you can't beat a travel agent for personalized service. If you need to change your itinerary or need help if you've been bumped off a flight, your travel agent can make the arrangements on your behalf. While on business trips, I've been able to call my agent to book me on a different flight when mine was cancelled or delayed, whereas I was unable to get help from the airline's customer-service department.

Discount Agents—Consolidators, brokers, discount travel agents. Call them what you will, but these are the Costco's of the travel industry. These companies purchase large blocks of airline seats, hotel rooms, tours, ferry tickets, and car rentals, and negotiate lower rates for bulk purchases. It's a high-volume, low-margin business that benefits you.

Consolidators will package a hotel stay along with your flight, and you'll get the whole package at a better discount than if the flight and hotel had been purchased separately. Discount brokers work similarly to consolidators in that they buy tickets in bulk from the airlines and pass the savings on to you, but they generally don't combine them with hotels or car rentals. You can purchase round-trip tickets, round-the-world tickets, circle-the-Pacific tickets, and many other combinations. While they may not call themselves consolidators or brokers in the yellow pages, you can find their ads in the travel section of newspapers and online, with prices that are less than what the airlines, search engines, and traditional travel agents offer.

My preferred method of locating a broker is to look through the Sunday travel section of major-market newspapers. Look week after week for the ones that consistently advertise. You'll want a reliable one that's going to be around for a while. Run the company's name through the Better Business Bureau's database (www.bbb.org) and buy with your credit card (even if it's a slightly higher cost) so that there's recourse if they go out of business without having sent your confirmation.

I have had hit-and-miss experiences with discount brokers. In one instance, the itinerary dates that they emailed me for confirmation were different than the dates for which I was subsequently ticketed. I had purchased by check (rather than credit card) to save on a surcharge and had no recourse either through the broker or the airline, even though I had proof the dates didn't match up. I went (to Greece) and had a lovely time, but I won't ever again use that company.

Seating Assignments

Always request your seating preference (aisle, window, or exit row) as early as possible, preferably when you're making your reservation. If you are a member of a frequent-flier program, provide this information when you book your flight. If you are part of an elite program, you could get upgraded to business or first class.

SeatGuru (www.seatguru.com) allows you to view seating charts by plane type, and makes recommendations on best seating options. On occasion, aircrafts and seating assignments change, so don't get too attached to that aisle seat.

Some airlines now charge for aisle and exit row seats or hold them for their elite members.

⚜ Boarding Passes

You can print your boarding pass up to 24 hours in advance of your departure. If you don't have bags to check, this allows you to go directly to security and pass by the ticket counter completely. If you do have bags to check, you can still avoid the ticket counter by leaving your bags at curbside check-in. There is a nominal fee for this (generally $2 per bag), but it will be worth it if there are long lines at the ticket counter.

If you aren't able to print out your boarding pass in advance, simply go to a kiosk at your airline's counter to print it out.

⚜ Airport Lounges

These are an oasis from the horde of travelers rushing to and from their gates. You can purchase a membership into these lounges through your preferred airline or join a membership club such as Priority Pass (www.prioritypass.com), which allows you access to a wide range of lounges around the world. Memberships start at about $100. These lounges often have free newspapers, wireless or high-speed Internet connections for your laptop, and free drinks and snacks. Most importantly, they are a place to relax in a quiet environment.

Hot Tip! If you're traveling abroad with first-class tickets, your airline may admit you into their lounge. Check directly at your airline's lounge reception area.

6.

THIS BED IS JUUUUST RIGHT

THERE'S *a delicate balance between finding the perfect fit between your comfort and your budget. While we'd all love to end each travel day in the feathery comfort of a Heavenly Bed by Westin, we travel knowing that sometimes interesting environments and unique opportunities (not to mention finances) don't equal comfort. You can maximize your travel experience to include unique and affordable accommodations by thoughtfully planning where you'll stay.*

⚘ Some Helpful Guidelines

As a solo female traveler, you'll want to base your choice of accommodation on the safety of its location, as well as on your budget and interests. Consider whether you wish to stay close to the city center or nearer to the airport (if you have an early-morning departure). As your needs and comfort level increase, your options get narrower.

Not all accommodations have a web presence, making it more difficult to book in advance. However, I do recommend you book your first night's stay, so you'll have a confirmed place to go once you arrive at the airport. Otherwise, you risk having a taxi or shuttle driver making recommendations for hotels where they may get a kickback.

Ask to see the room before you commit to staying there. If you have a confirmed reservation that you booked prior to arrival and you don't feel safe, don't hesitate to go elsewhere, even if you lose your deposit or the cost of one night's stay.

If you have made a reservation for your first night at a place that is pricier than where you would normally stay, once you've caught up on your rest you can venture out to look for a room that's more in your price range.

Hot Tip! Prior to checking in, make sure the air conditioning, fan or heat work, and that there's hot water available.

Except under rare circumstances, such as Diwali in India, and in very remote areas, there will always be a room available for you in a city or village if you can be flexible and open to new experiences. Mary, one stalwart traveler, stayed on the stone floor of a monastery in Aix-en-Provence, France, when every other hotel was booked due to an art show. Of course, she was awakened bright and early, and asked to leave before the monks stirred!

Regardless of the type of lodging, consider choosing a locally owned accommodation. Chris Torrison MacKay, who co-founded the community-based travel organization Crooked Trails (www.crookedtrails.com), suggests that it's "not cultur-ally sensitive staying at a Hilton. Stay in a locally owned guest house or B&B, and the family will invite you in. These are com-munity-based facilities where the locals are more involved."

Broadly speaking, the following accommodation types are listed in order of cost.

Resorts

Resorts are located in popular tourist spots such as beaches or ski areas, or near family attractions such as Disney World. Most include restaurants and shops, in addition to a wide va-riety of on-site activities, such as water sports and entertain-ment. They might be all-inclusive, with everything paid for up-front, or they may charge for anything beyond your room costs. Resorts can be expensive for solo travelers (particularly if they charge a single-supplement fee). However, you might find that staying at a resort is secure, an easy way to meet oth-ers, and a convenient way to book day trips, since they usually have tours available through their concierge service. Meals are generally available on-site, as are spa facilities.

Destination Spas

Destination spas set themselves apart from resorts in that they offer a full spa experience that may include fitness activities, such as yoga, nutritional classes, body treatments, and mind/

body educational classes. While accommodations, meals, and some classes are often included in the price, additional programs and treatments cost extra.

✲ Hotels

Of all the accommodation types, we're most familiar with hotels. However, even within this category, there's a wide range of choices. Chain hotels are usually a safe bet, though it's important to consider the location. One chain can have several hotels within a given city. If one is far less expensive than another, it may be located in an undesirable section of town. There's a good chance chain hotels won't be your most interesting option.

Many guidebooks categorize accommodations into low-, middle-, and high-price ranges, and provide information on how safe an area is. If you find that the area is filled with low-end restaurants and backpacker cafés or is near a railway station, it may be less safe than accommodations located even just a few blocks away.

Booking your first night's stay alleviates any stress related to finding a safe hotel, particularly if you're arriving at night. On a trip to Egypt, Sarah, a well-heeled traveler, arrived very late in the evening in Cairo and had a taxi driver take her to a hotel she had picked out of her guidebook. At one in the morning, however, the hotel was booked. "The taxi driver said he'd take me to his house, but I declined. Instead, I ended up in a totally sleazy, dirty place and couldn't sleep all night."

If you arrive at a destination without a plan of where to stay, you may find a tourist kiosk set up at the airport, train, or bus station where you can find accommodation suggestions. Or you can check with the local tourism office. Keep your eye open for message boards where tourists congregate, such as transit stations and Internet cafés.

Mary got creative during her Europe trip. "Once in a while when I arrived in a city, the place I had picked out from my guidebook would be full. When I looked around, I found the train station would have postings on message boards, or a guide for the city would direct me to a place to stay. Sometimes, old women sitting on the wall at the train station would walk me to their hotel. Lots of people with rooms to rent were waiting at train stations for tourists."

You may be more comfortable booking accommodations for your whole trip (if you know your itinerary), or you can book hotels a few days out via phone or Internet while traveling. Otherwise, you can always wing it as you go. While this can be much more fun, it can cause some stress if you arrive in a town with few lodging options.

Boutique hotels started cropping up in North America and around the world in the late 1980s. These are often quirky, sometimes expensive and usually independently owned hotels that are uniquely furnished around a theme or style. Simply search online for boutique hotels in the city you're visiting. The Pacific Palisades Hotel in Vancouver, British Columbia, for instance, features a penthouse with Jetson-style furniture and free Häagen-Dazs ice cream. Of course, I could run out to the store for my own pint, but how fabulous to have it delivered to my room!

If you have special needs, call the hotel directly to confirm they can accommodate your request (i.e. gym, pool, in-room Wi-Fi). If the hotel is part of a chain, their website may only provide generic information, and it may not correlate with your specific destination. I've booked hotels online only to find out that the gym facilities listed don't exist for that location.

Grab a business card or write down the name, address, and phone number of your hotel in case you get lost once you venture out. It also serves as an excellent way to provide your destination to a taxi or bus driver. I once got myself turned around while walking in the city of Oaxaca, Mexico. It took me an hour to find my hotel.

Hot Tip! If you're staying in a city, ask for a quiet room and one on an upper floor, as the view may be better. Always ask to see the room first before plunking down your credit card or cash.

Motels

Generally less expensive than hotels, motels (motor hotels) can be independently owned or part of a chain. They usually have doors that face out to the parking lot, allowing for anonymity in terms of interacting with the hotel staff. In cities, motels have a reputation for being located near seedier areas. Motels located in small towns are often family owned, and sometimes the only lodging option available.

Motels often aren't as safe for solo women travelers because the room doors open out to public areas. Always keep the deadbolt and chain locked on the door, and alert hotel staff immediately if you believe you are being watched.

Bed and Breakfasts

Bed and breakfasts are just that. Typically they are a single-family home or an inn with private rooms and are managed by the owners or caretakers living on-site or nearby. You get a private room (with a private or shared bathroom) and home-made breakfast in the morning. Slightly more expensive than a moderately priced hotel, a B&B provides you with a peek into the locals' lives. They are an excellent way to meet people since breakfast is often shared in a communal dining area. While these are located virtually worldwide, they are most common in North America and Europe.

🍂 Pensions

While not technically a bed and breakfast, pensions are usually small, family-run hotels that provide breakfast. They are most often found in Europe. While pensions may be light on amenities (no phone or TV, with a shared bathroom), these are a wonderful alternative to more expensive hotels. I found a pension in Rome that was quite charming. It was located down an unassuming side alley filled with outdoor cafés and fruit stands, and breakfast was served in a nicely finished basement, where I got to mingle with other guests.

🍂 Youth Hostels

More than 10,000 hostels around the world are registered with Hostelling International (HI, www.hihostels.com). Definitely not just for youths, these shared facilities are open to young and old alike. They are popular with European families and backpackers the world over because they are so affordable. You can stay in a room with shared bunks or ask if a private room is available. Some youth hostels impose curfews and require that you vacate the premises during the day while they are cleaned. However, they also include shared kitchens, which are not only a great place to meet other travelers, but will also help you cut down on food costs.

Rates vary depending on location, but they start at about $15 a night. A moderately priced membership will save you a few

6. THIS BED IS JUUUUST RIGHT

bucks per stay and can be purchased prior to your trip at the nearest hostel or, once you embark on your trip, directly from the first hostel at which you stay. Unfortunately, you cannot purchase a membership online.

In addition to hostels that are part of the HI network, there are unaffiliated hostels that may be too new to be part of the system, may not be quite up to the HI standards, or may choose to stay independent. Often these are listed in guidebooks, or you can find them by searching the Internet.

Depending on their location, some hostels will be a bit more raucous than others. You can bet that the hostel on Cairn's Esplanade in Australia, with its 24-hour access and nearby nightlife scene will attract a rowdier group of people than the Cape Clear Island (eight miles by boat) hostel in Ireland. If it's peace and quiet you need, reference the HI website and email or call the hostel itself to determine if the location will suit your needs.

Student dorm housing at universities is sometimes rented out in the summer to travelers. These summer hostels are primarily located in northern Europe; they can be found by searching online for your destination.

Hot Tip! Carry a sleep sack and pillowcase to use at any accommodation with questionable bedding. Shaped like a sleeping bag, a sleep sack is made from cotton or silk, packs away rather easily, and is required at many youth hostels. You can easily purchase them online, or you can buy or rent one directly from a hostel.

❧ YMCAs

The Young Men's Christian Association (YMCA) may be one of the very last places you would think to stay. However, YMCAs throughout the world can accommodate women travelers in private and dorm settings (though not all YMCAs have lodging facilities). Prices vary depending on location. The YMCA's international website (www.ymca.int) includes worldwide listings.

I first became aware of the ability to stay at a Y during my Central American trip. These were a very affordable option for me in towns where there was no youth hostel. In one instance, I was the only person staying at the Y, and I paid less than $3 for a night's stay.

✾ Home Swaps and Homestays

Home swaps and homestays allow you to live with and among the locals, whether it's a week-long swap or an overnight.

If you're traveling for a week or more, you can offer your home in exchange for staying elsewhere. This is an affordable way to stay in one place for a period of time beyond just a few nights. Some home-swap programs to check on include HomeExchange. com (www.homeexchange.com), Intervac Home Exchange (www.intervacus.com), Seniors Home Exchange (www. seniorshomeexchange.com) and Green Theme International Home Exchange (www.gti-home-exchange.com).

Couchsurfing (www.couchsurfing.com) and GlobalFreeloaders (www.globalfreeloaders.com) are websites in which you can meet and agree to host other travelers, and find a free place to stay during your journey. Accommodations vary tremendously, and can range from simply sleeping on someone's couch to having home-cooked meals provided. You introduce yourself through the website and make a request to stay with a potential host. No private information is provided by the websites. The guest and host take the responsibility of sharing their contact information themselves. As a solo woman traveler, you'll want to be extra cautious when communicating with strangers. Ask for references from other travelers who have stayed with your host, and never feel obligated to stay where you feel the slightest bit uncomfortable.

✥ Farm Vacations

If you're eager to experience country living and you don't mind rolling up your sleeves for a bit of work, try staying on a farm. The best-known farm-vacation program is WWOOF, World-Wide Opportunities on Organic Farms (www.wwoof.org). Organic host farms around the world welcome travelers for short stays in exchange for light manual labor. Depending on the time of year, you may have no chores or you may spend four to six hours of your day picking strawberries or doing other tasks. Outside the WWOOF program, other farm stays are available around the world; search online for specific destinations.

✥ Campgrounds

Camping can be a relatively inexpensive way to travel. Campsites range from primitive, undeveloped sites where there may be only a pit toilet with no electricity hookup or running water, to dedicated campsites with full hookups (water, sewage, electric for RVs). Campsites are readily found throughout the Americas, Europe, and Africa, and while Asia is a bit light on the opportunities, camping in India is quite possible. Prices will range from free to upwards of $30 per night if you're staying at a facility with a pool, restaurant, and grocery store.

Many countries, including Europe, New Zealand, and Australia, allow for informal camping, in which you can pitch your tent (perhaps in a field) as long as you attempt to seek permission from the nearest homeowners. While staying in a youth hostel in New Orleans, I met many Kiwis and

Brits who were astounded that they couldn't just head out to rural communities and sleep in their tent on someone's farmland without consequence.

While riding my motorcycle through Central America, I made a conscious decision not to camp along the way. I felt that it was too risky as a female traveling solo through a high-machismo region to overnight in areas where it was obvious that I was on my own. There are many places in the world, however, where I would feel more comfortable camping without companions. As a matter of fact, I've traveled around the United States and up the Alcan Highway to Alaska, staying in campgrounds without incidence.

Laura quickly learned one of the best means to staying safe while camping during her numerous solo motorcycle trips. "I was pretty concerned the first time I camped on my own. I learned to make friends with the old folks in the RV next door, and half the time they'd bring me coffee in the morning."

Campgrounds are usually located in remote areas, so you would need your own car to get there, or you would need to hike from a drop-off point, such as a bus stop.

For tips on packing your camping gear, see Chapter 10, Pack it Up.

❄ Hut-to-hut Systems

For skiers and hikers, there's nothing more rewarding than traversing the woods from hut to hut to maximize your outdoor experience. From British Columbia to Slovakia, trail systems link "huts," which can be anything from rustic shacks to beautiful lodges. These trail systems offer not only exquisite scenery, but also the chance to meet locals and other outdoors-oriented people.

This type of outdoor recreation may even eliminate the need for you to carry your tent, sleeping bag, and cooking gear, lightening your load considerably. Before setting out, find out what you can expect from the huts where you'll be staying, and pack accordingly.

Alison, an experienced hiker and climber, took an organized 10-day tour through the Alps and didn't know anyone before she left home. "We stayed in huts along the route, but the term 'huts' is pretty loose. Most of the accommodations were hotels, with linen service and restaurants."

While there are hut-to-hut systems in North America (Colorado, in particular), they are especially popular in Europe. The European hut systems originated to deter people from camping in wilderness areas. The systems help control potential overuse of the land, and they are conveniently situated a day's hike or ski apart. Inquire with the nearest Alpine club (by searching online) in the countries you are visiting, as they own and operate many of the huts. They can provide specific information, as well as books and pamphlets mapping the hiking routes.

7.

GETTIN' AROUND

ONCE *you've hit the road, it will be time to decide just how you're going to get yourself around within the country or region in which you're traveling. Most likely there will be lots of options from which to choose. You'll want to consider comfort, cost, and your schedule when making your choices.*

🎵 Trains

There's something romantic about the clack, clack, clack and slight shifting of the rail car as you watch the landscape roll by. Rather than being plunked down at your destination's airport, the slower pace of a train allows you to experience the gradual change in scenery.

In most developed countries, traveling by train is quite comfortable and safe for solo women travelers.

In countries with extensive rail lines, taking the train can be more affordable than flying, and it's often faster than buses and/or cars. Since you have the ability to walk around and stretch while traveling on a train, it can be more comfortable than other forms of transportation. And many trains offer sleeper cars. Some trains even provide sleeper cars dedicated to females.

Except during very busy times, such as holidays and festivals, tickets can be purchased just prior to or even on your departure date; although, if I have to be somewhere by a certain time and date, I book in advance. As some cities have more than one station location, be sure to confirm which one you'll arrive in when you purchase your ticket.

In less-developed areas, you may want to book first-class passage or a private berth if your wallet allows. Train tickets in these countries will be relatively affordable and will provide you with a bit more safety than traveling in often overcrowded second- or third-class cars.

One of the most vivid memories I have of traveling through India was when a young boy stepped on the train at a rural stop and sang his heart out in a hauntingly beautiful language that I couldn't understand. He was no more than nine, but he belted out that tune as if his life depended on it. And it might have. Between breaths, he collected small coins from passengers until the next stop, where he disembarked.

Rail Passes—Good for use in 18 countries (excluding the U.K.), Eurail passes are geared toward non-European travelers and, as a result, it is difficult to find an outlet where you can purchase them in Europe. While the Eurail Aid offices located in major European cities do sell them, they are priced at a 20 percent markup. As a result, it's best to purchase online in advance at the Eurail website (www.eurail.com). The pass will be good for a specified time period, and doesn't go into effect until your first day of travel.

Eurail Pass Flexi allows you to travel during a specified time period on nonconsecutive days. While in Europe, Mary traveled extensively on her Flexi pass. "If I overnighted on the train, I could use it for two days on one punch." In other words, since travel after 7 p.m. counts toward the following day, Mary was able to travel one evening and all the next day using up only one day's travel on her pass. Traveling overnight also allowed her to forego the cost of a hotel for the evening.

Use your rail pass only for longer, more expensive, trips. If you're traveling within a small region, such as the northwest corner of Italy, I recommend buying point-to-point tickets, rather than using a rail pass.

Other passes, such as the Britrail Pass, must be purchased in advance outside of the country you'll be traveling in, and validated on your first day of travel, no more than six months from date of purchase. For detailed info on purchasing rail tickets for all of Europe, including the U.K. and Australia, go to the RailPass website (www.railpass.com).

While the Eurail pass may be the most well-known, rail passes are also available for trains in Japan, India, Australia, New Zealand, and parts of Africa. You can often purchase combination passes that include rail and bus, or rail and ferry services.

Thomas Cook timetables provide complete listings of train schedules throughout the world. To better plan your schedule, purchase schedules for Europe or overseas from the Thomas Cook website (www.thomascookpublishing.com).

❦ Ship and Ferries

Taking a ferry from the island of Santorini, Greece, to the island of Crete, I watched from the deck as the sun slowly set. The sky was on fire, lit in reds and pinks. The island slowly disappeared as the boat pushed on into the Aegean Sea.

No mode of transportation can compare with being on water, and unless you're landlocked, plan at least a small part of your journey on a boat, ship, catamaran, dinghy, long-tail boat, or skiff. (I suggest skipping the lifeboat.)

The necessity to book tickets for in-state, in-country, and intercountry ferry systems varies. Washington State has a vast route of ferries in which no advanced purchase is necessary for most sailings (as a matter of fact, it's first come, first served). For ferries in general, however, tickets are normally required in advance for longer-distance sailings (when you will want a private sleeping berth) and shorter sailings when you need a confirmed seat.

Major ferry systems often allow online booking. The FAQ sections on each ferry system's website should answer your questions as to whether it's possible to book in advance, whether you can book online, and what your chances are of getting tickets if you plan to purchase just prior to departure.

Unless you're traveling during high season, you'll find it easy to book your tickets for short-distance boat rides just days in advance (if not the same day). Of course, if you must be in a city for a specific event, the farther ahead you book, the more you can rest easy that you'll arrive on time.

Purchase your tickets directly from the ferry company, as travel and booking agents will tack on additional charges to cover their services. However, there are times when it may be well worth having someone else handle ticketing on your be-half, especially if you don't speak the language.

Cars

Some countries—jeez, some regions in North America—may have very different driving habits than you're used to, not to mention that they may drive on the other side of the road. After his having clipped the side-view mirror on a parked car in Sydney, my boss let me drive during a business trip Down Under. No doubt he was generally a good driver, but it does take time getting used to driving on the other side of the road and shifting with your left hand.

Travel forums and guidebooks will give you a good general idea as to what to expect when driving in another country. In Central America, for example, drivers use their blinkers to in-dicate when it's safe for you to pass them. While most driv-ers in Texas will stay in the passing lane no matter how fast or slow they are going, in countries such as Germany and France, you will learn to always stay in the slow lane unless you plan to practice for a road race or want to get run over by an ap-proaching BMW or Renault.

Your Own Vehicle—Before your trip, enroll in a roadside-assistance program such as AAA in the United States or CAA in Canada. In addition to offering towing service if you break down, these associations provide maps, tour books, travel accessories, and auto and health insurance. They are the perfect remedy if Prince (or Princess) Charming doesn't come to your rescue.

I can't recommend these services highly enough. My car was once stuck in the middle of a downtown intersection. Suspecting that such a thing might happen to my car sooner, rather than later, I had purchased an AAA membership just weeks before. I called from a local shop, and AAA came to the rescue rather quickly to tow away my poor vehicle.

To ensure the safest driving journey for yourself, you'll want everything tuned up and in good working order prior to your trip. I also recommend buying the appropriate repair or owner's manual for your car.

Familiarize yourself with all the necessary equipment to change a tire, and be prepared with flares and basic tools. If you're like me, you can't tell the difference between a set of metric and U.S. standard tools. That doesn't stop me from at least tinkering around to attempt to figure out what the problem might be. If you can't fix it yourself, there are always those roadside-assistance programs to help out.

Rentals—Whether traveling to New Jersey or Paris, I book my car rental as far in advance as possible. The closer to your travel date, the more expensive the rental typically is, as fewer cars are available (economy cars sell out first) and the rental agencies know you need their services. Fortunately, few rental companies require that you guarantee your rental with a credit card. This gives you the opportunity to book your car and then shop around or even re-book with the same company if their rates go down.

Renting off-site is cheaper than renting directly at the airport, as there are additional taxes involved if the agency is located at the terminal.

Of course, you can book at the last minute or directly at a rental counter, but chances are that you'll pay more if you haven't compared costs. You may have several rental agencies to choose from once you land. I've walked to a couple of different rental counters at an airport to see who would give me the best deal by mentioning lower quotes from other agents.

When renting a car, thoroughly scrutinize it for dents and scratches before you leave the lot. I've rented cars in Amarillo that were damaged by hailstorms and cars in New Jersey that had dents and scratches. Even if it means I have to go back inside to the rental counter, it's important to report any issues that could come back to haunt me upon returning the vehicle.

Check the gas to make sure you're leaving the lot with a completely full tank. If it's not full, require that they fill it up or indicate the gas level on your paperwork. With the high price of gas, you do not want to get stuck paying for someone else's trip! Don't forget to return the car with a full tank. On my way out of the airport, I make note of the nearest gas station, so I can easily fill up upon my return. I learned that after many trips of having to backtrack from the airport to find the nearest pump.

In some countries, such as Myanmar, it's impossible to rent (or even legally drive) a car as a foreigner. If traveling in these countries, you will be required to hire a driver through a local tour company, or you may be able to find a private citizen who's willing to take on the job.

Hot Tip! Most cars available for rent outside of North America are manual transmissions, meaning you'll need to know how to drive a stick shift. Don't plan to learn on foreign roads!

Shuttles

Ground transportation can eat into your budget quite quickly. Help save on some of these costs by checking with your hotel for a free pick-up service from the airport, train, or bus station. If your hotel doesn't offer such a perk, try a private shuttle, rather than paying for a taxi. Many shuttle services have websites on which you can arrange for a pickup in advance; or ask at a transportation help desk once you arrive at your destination. While the shuttle may take a circuitous route to your lodging, because you'll be sharing a ride with others, it can easily be half the cost of a taxi.

If you book in advance, call or email the shuttle company ahead of time so you know where to find the service when you arrive.

Taxis

If a taxi is your only option—whether it's to and from the airport or between destinations—always ask for the cost up front, and be sure you and the driver are clear about the price. (15 and 50 can sound a lot alike.) Don't be shy about asking other travelers who are lingering about the taxi stand to share a ride with you.

Many times, taxis that are just outside of the main drag of the airport are a lot less expensive than those found in an airport arrival area. Your guidebook will give you some tips on where to find the best deals. When flying into Puerto Vallarta, Mexico, for example, you can easily save about one-third of the cost by walking across the street from the airport to the local taxi stand.

Buses

A bus ride doesn't hold nearly the romantic appeal that trains or boats do, but in countries (such as the United States) where the train system is not at all well connected, buses may be your most economical point-to-point option. If you're planning to travel a long distance via bus, book in advance and get to the terminal early to ensure a good seat (an aisle in the front) if seats aren't pre-assigned.

Short commuter-type trips within a city are first come, first served. Be prepared to stand during peak operating times and carry the exact fare, as most drivers won't give you change.

Many cities (and rural areas with spectacular scenery) offer sightseeing tours by bus. These will take you to the main sights in the area. It's an excellent way to be ushered around and see all the highlights without having to rent a car. You'll even have the opportunity to meet lots of folks.

Bicycles

With bikes, you can explore a city or the countryside without being dependent on public transportation. If you're a bike enthusiast, consider planning an entire trip, or a portion of one, using pedal power. You can take your own or rent by the day or week, depending on your itinerary, and choose to go it completely alone. Or you can join a guided bicycling tour.

For day use, obviously, you may find bicycles for rent at bike shops, but youth hostels and other accommodations could very well have bikes for hire (or free). Loads of websites list companies that rent bicycles around the world. Book in advance to ensure the availability of a bike that fits your height. Many companies have panniers and trailers available for rent, and will even deliver the bike to your hotel.

Beverly uses her bicycle as her primary mode of transportation throughout the world, including five trips around Bolivia. She admits that when traveling solo, it's difficult with too much stuff. "You can ship your gear domestically in the United States to bike shops, as long as you arrange it with the shop in advance. If you check your bike on an airline, you can ship it in a bike box. Or you could buy a Bike Friday." Bike Fridays, by the way, are collapsible bikes. More information on these can be found at the Bike Friday website (www.bikefriday.com).

🪕 Motorcycles

Laura has covered a good portion of North America and Europe by motorcycle. "I love traveling alone on a motorcycle. I think part of it is I'm completely accessible. I'm not a big old guy with a grizzly beard in stitched leathers. Everybody has a secret fantasy to ride a bike, and I end up meeting a lot of people."

If traveling by motorcycle, you have the option of shipping your bike to a destination to begin the journey (in Europe or South Africa, for example), or you can rent a bike once you arrive. If renting, carrying your own gear (helmet, leathers, chaps, raingear, gloves, etc.) is a must for maximum comfort and safety. It's unlikely that your insurance company will cover a rental or even riding your own motorcycle in a foreign country, but they may be able to direct you to insurance providers at your destination.

If you choose to go solo, you can certainly plan all the details yourself. I rode a BMW F650 solo from Seattle to Panama during a nine-week trip. While I had a lot of people supporting me emotionally and with some of the details, I planned the route, found my own hotels, restaurants, and grocery stores, arranged for additional travel insurance, and worked with a shipping company to get the bike back home. (You didn't think I'd ride all the way back, did you?)

For Laura, there's no other way to travel. "If I stop at a campground and something freaks me out, like there's only one other camper and it's a strange guy, I can get back on my bike and ride 20 miles to the next campground. If you're on a bicycle, you can't do that. I don't analyze my gut; if it doesn't feel right, I leave."

Anytime you're driving your own vehicle in unfamiliar territory, particularly a motorcycle, never drive at night. It's best to leave first thing in the morning, take a break for lunch, and spend time in the early afternoon getting settled into your accommodation. This frees you up for sightseeing in the afternoon and early evening. I will admit to being lost after dark in Nicaragua trying to make my way to Granada. When I asked directions at a gas station, locals crammed in a car with a license plate lit up with multicolored light bulbs and motioned to me to follow them. I'm convinced that they got me even more lost. I somehow made my way safely into this quaint village, but I never let that happen again.

I did find that riding 200 to 300 miles a day was ideal for me and my posterior.

If you choose to go with a motorcycle tour company, it can make all of your arrangements, including shipping the bike to and from your starting point, mapping out a route, and arranging all hotels, meals, guides, and entertainment. Globe Riders (www.globeriders.com) specializes in small-group, long-duration tours through far-off corners of the world. Definitely for the adventurous. Iberian Moto Tours (www.imtbike.com), based in Madrid, specializes in tours through Spain and Morocco, and MotoDiscovery (www.motodiscovery.com) specializes in Central America with tours that include both on- and off-road riding.

ᨑ Local Transportation

Be sure to take advantage of local modes of transportation on your journey. In developing countries, these local services are part of the tourism industry's backbone. Residents depend on your dollars to feed their families, and in exchange they'll provide you with a lift on one of these charming forms of transportation.

Many of them are motorized (*bemos, collectivos, tuk tuks,* motorbikes), while others are pedal-powered (rickshaws, *cyclos*). You'll feel exhilarated zooming along Bangkok's streets in an open-aired tuk tuk or slowly plying the streets of Beijing in a pedicab. You're wide open to the smells (both good and bad) and sounds, and you're directly supporting the driver.

Always negotiate a fee up front, especially if the meter isn't working properly or is nonexistent. Write the price down and be clear what currency you're talking about.

On a trip to Bali, I was feeling weary and longing for a comfortable ride across the island from the airport to Ubud, some 30 miles away. While I hoped for an air-conditioned shuttle with a group of English-speaking tourists, I missed the last one and wound up tucked into the back of a bemo, an open-end pick-up truck with a group of women returning from the market. Holding bags of produce and live chickens, they boarded while I moved and scrunched until I had very little room left to sit on a hard bench.

I loved that ride. To this day, I can remember my hesitancy in jumping into the back of a truck with a group of people with whom I couldn't communicate. And I remember the thrill that came from feeling the wind in my hair and seeing the smiles that were shared as I shifted and moved my backpack, and they shifted and moved their day's purchases so we could all have a little more personal space.

8.

RED TAPE AND FORMALITIES

WHILE *it's natural to want your journey to be easygoing and filled with fun, it takes organization for things to work smoothly. Certainly, the preparation is more exciting when the end result involves a beach chair or ski slope. Regardless of your trip's final destination, there are still visas, itineraries, and directions to secure. Handling the details up front will allow you to relax on the road.*

✆ Passports

If traveling outside your own country, it's nearly always the case that you'll need a valid passport. While "valid" strictly means that your passport is good until the date of expiration, the country you're visiting will have its own requirements for how long before your passport expires. For instance, Costa Rica requires that your passport is valid for three months beyond your date of entry. Also, have at least four blank pages available. If you're flying, not meeting one or both of these requirements could cause you to be denied boarding; if you're crossing overland you could be turned away from a border.

If you are a U.S. citizen applying for a passport for the first time, submit your paperwork at one of 7,000 locations across the country (www.iafdb.travel.state.gov) and expect a six-week turnaround. Passports are valid for 10 years. To apply, you'll need to supply completed forms found on this website, two identical passport photographs of yourself, and a government-issued ID, such as a driver's license.

Canadians can apply for a passport that is valid for five years at a local passport office listed on the Passport Canada website (www.ppt.gc.ca). Fill out the appropriate forms, provide two identical photos, and have a guarantor complete and sign the designated portion of your paperwork.

If you are a citizen outside North America, check with your home country's guidelines.

If you're renewing your passport, U.S. citizens can do so via mail by sending form DS-82 along with your most recent passport, two passport photos, and funds to cover the fee to the National Passport Center. All info (and a downloadable form) is listed on the U.S. Department of State website. Canadian passports are not renewable, although you can apply for a new one using an online application or you can mail in form PPTC 004, which is downloadable from the Passport Canada site.

Passports can be expedited for an additional fee and extra shipping charges.

Your passport is the most valuable item you'll carry with you when you travel. Keep copies of the front page both at home and in your luggage. Some countries require that hotels register guests with the police, and will ask for your passport as ID. While this is standard procedure, the U.S. government recommends you retrieve your passport the next morning. If possible, leave a copy of the passport, rather than the original.

If you lose your passport while traveling abroad, immediately contact the local authorities and the nearest embassy or consulate for your country. The replacement process will go much more smoothly if you have a copy of your passport. If your passport is lost or stolen while you are at home, alert your passport agency and apply for a new one.

Susan, the kayaker, says that when she's on her own, it's far easier to take care of her important documents. "I feel less distracted because there's no one else's needs that I have to attend to."

🔖 Visas

A visa is a stamp in your passport or a piece of documentation that gives you permission to enter a country for a set number of days. Many countries require that you apply for a visa before arriving at the airport, while others will stamp your passport with a visa once you arrive. Guidebooks will have detailed information about each country's requirements, or you can go to the embassy or consulate website for the country you'll be visiting.

8. RED TAPE AND FORMALITIES

ҟ҈ҟ҈ҟ҈ Lenora's Story ҉ҟ҉ҟ҉ҟ

I traveled for 12 years on business all over the U.S. and to Bangkok, Rome, Tuscany, Paris, London, Frankfurt, Taipei, and Spain. My salvation was scheduling extra time to experience the culture. When traveling to Milan, which is like Manhattan, I would take a train north to Lake Maggiore, in Stresa, after I completed my business, and stay in this tiny resort town. I would take walks and just travel around by little boats to the islands on the lake.

In Mediterranean countries, I enjoyed getting to know the factory owners and their families, and I wasn't so interested in sightseeing. They want you in their homes and want you to meet their families, whereas in Asia, they want to take you out to nice restaurants.

The biggest thing about travel is that you have to be organized. You have to always be thinking ahead. When does my flight leave? When does the shuttle pick me up? Do I have enough tip money? How much do I tip? Do I have small change? What are the local customs? Planning is easier than winging it. And the ones who tend to get their pockets picked are the ones who look disheveled and unorganized.

If the country you plan to visit requires a visa, it can be obtained from the country's embassy in your country of residence or at their embassy elsewhere if you are already traveling. In some instances, your travel may be restricted and no visa obtained due to strained relationships between countries (the United States and Cuba, for instance).

If you are visiting a country that allows you to arrive at the airport without a visa, you may be granted fewer days' stay than if you had applied in advance. You may be able to extend your visa by showing proof that your finances can last through your intended length of stay. Take bank statements with you if there's a possibility you need to extend your visa, or make sure someone at home has access to the info, so they can fax, email, or mail it to you. I provided the Australian government with bank statements in which I had a shared account with "me Mum" when I applied for a threemonth visa extension. It worked. I had no intention of tapping into that account, but I was able to stay longer (and continue working under the table).

⚜ Vehicles

If you are driving a vehicle beyond your own borders, you'll need a valid driver's license, registration, insurance, and proof-of-ownership records. Your passport will be stamped to show that you've entered with a vehicle, and you won't be able to leave the country unless you drive it out, show that you've sold it (and paid appropriate taxes), or have proof that it was shipped out of the country on your behalf.

Make sure all your documentation is current. I had inadvertently let my driver's license expire two days prior to a business trip to New Jersey. I didn't even realize it until the rental-car agency pointed it out. Luckily, they turned a blind eye to my blunder and let me rent the car anyway. Phew.

When traveling abroad, it's a good idea to take an international driver's license, which can easily be purchased at your local AAA or CAA office by showing your current driver's license. Even if it is not required, the international license includes information translated into many languages, in the event you need to show it to authorities in another country. It can make life a lot easier.

✺ Phone/Contact List

Carry emergency contact names and phone numbers, and leave them in an obvious spot in your luggage. If something happens to you, a hotel staff person or the police will be able to notify your family or friends quickly.

Also, keep a separate list of people you want to stay in touch with on the road. If you're carrying a cell phone or laptop with contact information, make sure you have up-to-date phone numbers, addresses, and emails for everyone; otherwise, update a good old-fashioned sheet of paper.

✺ Reservations and Itineraries

Keep confirmation numbers for everything you've booked in advance. This includes hotels, shuttles, rental cars, and tours. Reservations can easily get lost within a company's system. Having a printed copy will aid you if there's a discrepancy with the cost or a question about the existence of the reservation.

After flying into Paris once, I realized that I had forgotten to print out the confirmation for the shuttle picking me up, and could not remember the name of the company. I assumed that someone would be waiting for me with my name scrawled on a sign. No luck.

I got over the fact that I was a fool for not being better prepared, hunted down an Internet café in the airport, retrieved the reservation number from my email, and called the company. They had been waiting outside the arrival area the whole time. No big sign. No fanfare that I had landed safely. Just a patient man wondering why my flight might have been delayed.

Photocopy all important documents, such as passports, airplane tickets (if you don't have e-tickets saved in your email), travelers checks, visas, and credit cards, and leave them where a friend or family member at home can access them if need be.

If you're traveling for business, assume that you won't have access to a printer while on the road, and print out all your important documents the day before departure, keeping them in a folder in order of when you'll need them.

❧ Photocopy all of the following:

- Flight reservation or e-tickets
- Boarding passes (which can be printed out as early as 24 hours in advance)
- Car-rental reservation
- Shuttle reservation (if not renting a car)
- Directions to your hotel from the airport
- Hotel reservation
- Directions to restaurants from both the hotel and airport (in case you want to stop on the way to your hotel)
- Directions to business or other meetings
- Directions back to the airport (if you're renting a car)

Hot Tip! You could put that all-in-one printer/copier/scanner to use by scanning important documents and then emailing them to yourself. If you've lost your passport on a trek in Nepal, you'll be able to access it at an Internet café in Kathmandu, saving you loads of time, money, and migraines.

❀ Bills

Prior to leaving home, pay your bills, mortgage, rent, and car payments, or set up an automated bill-payer to handle these. For a low-tech solution, you can prepare your bills, place them in pre-stamped and dated envelopes, and have a friend drop them in the mail as they come due. Obviously, choose a person you know is reliable. On one trip, I left my prepared bills with a boyfriend. I came home to find the un-mailed envelopes exactly where I had left them. Arrrggghhh.

Hot Tip! Before you travel, call your credit-card companies and let them know to which countries you'll be traveling. This way, they'll accept the foreign charges and won't assume that your card has been stolen and freeze your account.

If you plan on paying a credit-card bill by phone (by providing your bank account number) while you're out of the country, use the company's non-toll-free number and call collect. There is often an additional charge to pay by phone, but it'll do in a pinch if you can't access your account online and have forgotten to make a payment. I got dinged $15 by Visa while on a trip to Central America. Better than it being a late payment.

❀ Prescriptions and Medical Records

Even if you have enough medication to last your entire trip, it doesn't hurt to have a backup prescription in case you lose your meds. Medications can often be easily refilled at a local pharmacy. While there has been a lot of brouhaha over the safety of medications purchased overseas, it's my personal (and very humble) opinion that this fear is propagated by U.S. government regulators, and is not necessarily founded in reality.

Carry your eyeglass or contact prescription, as well. You might find that you can pick up a spare pair of eyeglasses in an area where they are far more affordable than in your own country. And if you break or lose yours along the way, you can easily get them replaced without an exam.

For any preexisting conditions you may have, take any necessary medical records. This could save days in having to wait for the information to be faxed from your doctor's office. And, if you have had vaccinations for the journey, carry your yellow health card (discussed in more detail in Chapter 9, Staying Healthy on the Road).

9.

STAYING HEALTHY ON THE ROAD

STAYING *healthy during your journey is more than just eating right along the way. Prepare your body by getting into shape and getting appropriate vaccinations prior to your departure. And be sure to take along prophylaxes. Prepare yourself mentally and emotionally, by knowing what to do in advance if you have a medical emergency.*

⚘ Health and Travel Insurance

Check your insurance policy, as you may be covered for emergency and urgent care needs while traveling. Some providers will reimburse you once you've paid out of pocket. Government programs such as Medicare, however, generally do not cover care outside your country of residence. If you do have coverage, keep in mind that it might not include activities such as adventure sports or riding a motorcycle.

Hot Tip! Even if your medical insurance doesn't cover international travel, keep your insurance card with you in case you need it to and from your destination.

If you do not have health insurance that's valid overseas, the U.S. Department of State website has a list of U.S. and internationally based travel-insurance providers (under the Health Issues section).

Travel insurance can provide you with a variety of benefits. To name a few, you can be covered for trip cancellation or delays, lost luggage, and emergency medical and health expenses (including evacuation). It can also pay benefits in the case of an accidental death.

If you've shelled out a heap of money for a tour package or non-refundable hotel or plane tickets, consider travel insurance. For a relatively small fee, you'll be reimbursed in the event you have to cancel your trip. Depending on the policy, other benefits may include baggage reimbursement, medical, dental, and evacuation. Visit Insure My Trip (www.insuremytrip. com) to compare prices from about 20 different providers.

Evacuation insurance can ensure transportation to a medical facility in the case of a serious accident or illness in which you don't want to be treated by the local hospital. For example, you would want to be taken to the nearest city with Western-trained doctors, or perhaps even home, in the case of a severely broken bone. The cost for such a departure can easily top $60,000. With evacuation insurance, you would be responsible for your deductible and little, if anything, else.

I have purchased both MEDEX (www.medexassist.com) and Medjet Assist (www.medjetassistance.com). Though I've never had to use either (thank goodness!), the process of signing up can be done in literally minutes. The cost is a fraction of the amount of your entire trip (less than $100 for a one-month trip for a person in her 40s), and minor compared to the potential out-of-pocket expenses incurred in the case of an accident. It's also well worth the additional cost to have peace of mind.

As a tour guide, Betty Ann learned first hand how important travel insurance can be. While guiding a tour on Easter Island, one of the most remote islands in the world, one of the tour members became gravely ill. "A medevac plane was dispatched from San Francisco with a medical staff of four. The cost was $97,000 (an amount the patient actually wrote a check for), and he was, luckily, reimbursed by his travel insurance company."

Marlene Fedin, who runs the website Wellness Concierge (www.wellnessconcierge.com), emphatically states, "Get evacuation insurance, because if you're abroad and get hurt, it can cost a bloody fortune to get you to a better hospital or out of the country."

9. STAYING HEALTHY ON THE ROAD

༄༄༄ Jo's Story ༄༄༄

I had just crossed the Sahara, from Tunis to Cotonou, and was on my way to Timbuktu when a moment's inattention in the dark landed me in a drainage ditch.

I was in Accra, Ghana, walking through a crowd of people at a bus stop, and didn't see the yawning ditch crossing my path. The concrete ditch had a knife-sharp edge, and my left foot caught on it as I fell. The ditch was narrow and if I had hit the other edge with my chest or neck I would have been killed, but I took a 90-degree turn in the fall, had a soft landing in the muck, and (I thought) not a scratch on me. However, when two young men helped me up onto the rim, I saw that my foot was just hanging.

The guys flagged down a taxi and took me to a teaching hospital, the largest hospital in West Africa. I had travel insurance and was equipped with an 800 number, but that didn't work. Then I tried to call collect. But because of fraud, no collect calls are allowed from Ghana to the United States. So, at 10 p.m., one of my rescuers went to find a telephone card to purchase. Then they wheeled me on a gurney to a pay phone out in the hospital grounds to finally contact the insurance company and tell them of my plight.

As long as this was just a broken ankle, I was content to have it fixed in Ghana, and would then continue my trip on crutches. However, a couple of days after a third surgery I noticed seepage around the bandages, which was attracting flies. The hospital's remedy was to just add more bandages until the surgeon was due to come and remove the bandages the following day. When they did come off it was clear to me that I was in deep trouble, and started the proceedings to be evacuated to London, thinking that my $60,000 in travel insurance would stretch farther there than in the United States.

I came to find out that once back at home (in the United States) there is no further coverage, regardless of where the accident occurred.

Due to the bureaucracy in the hospital, it took three days to get them to confirm to the insurance company that I should be returned to care in the West. I had an unidentified infection—later found to be a fecal infection—contracted in the ditch, so travel on a commercial airliner was not considered appropriate. An air ambulance was sent from Frankfurt, pilot, and co-pilot, doctor, and nurse on board. An ambulance was waiting for me on the tarmac at Heathrow, which arrived at Charing Cross Hospital at 1 a.m. on Christmas Eve.

One week of hospitalization in Ghana and five weeks of hospitalization in London, all as a private patient, with a total of six surgeries, totaled $61,400, so I had a total of just $1,400 to pay for the whole escapade, plus my annual insurance premium of $360. The cost of the evacuation was not counted as part of the $60,000 coverage, and instead, was completely covered. The best investment I have ever made. The lesson of all this is "Don't leave home without it!"

I believe that everything happens for a reason, and if I had not been brought up short by the accident, I would have walked into a rapidly deteriorating civil war in Côte D'Ivoire. Life is for living, not staying safely at home. I finally made it to Timbuktu three years later, mobility impaired, but I made it!

❦ Your Medicine and Prescriptions

If you're like most people, you'll have some health issues to deal with on the road, such as allergic reactions, intestinal issues, physical challenges, or other problems to which you must pay special attention. Don't allow these issues to prevent you from traveling, but know your limitations and be prepared with remedies and medicines for your specific predispositions.

If you carry prescription drugs, keep them in their original packaging and take copies of the prescriptions. The copies will not only verify your need for the medication if you're questioned by authorities, but you'll be able to get a refill if you run out or lose your medication along the way.

Prepare a medical bio sheet that includes detailed info on your health, medications, and allergies. Include the names and phone numbers of your physicians and family members to contact in an emergency. As an alternative, MedicalSummary (www.medicalsummary.com) allows you to store, retrieve, and update your personal medical records online. It also allows you to print a card summarizing your medical information so that you can easily carry it with you. MedicAlert (www.medicalert.com) allows you to keep your medical records on a USB-supported keychain-like device, allowing healthcare providers to have immediate access to your medical history.

❦ Immunizations

It's extremely important to educate yourself about what diseases and viruses you might encounter in your travels. According to Marlene, who runs the website Wellness Concierge (www.wellnessconcierge.com), "Just being aware of diseases such as malaria and West Nile virus won't make them go away, but you should know what to do."

Create Your Own First-Aid Kit

- Sunscreen
- Antihistamine
- Decongestant
- Pain & fever medication
- Mosquito repellent
- Acetaminophen
- Ibuprofen
- Mild laxative
- Antidiarrheal
- Cough drops

- Antifungal & antibacterial ointments
- Hydrocortisone cream
- Bandages
- Tweezers
- Alcohol wipes
- Blister kit
- Cotton swabs
- Tissues

Point well taken. The Centers for Disease Control and Prevention website (www.cdc.gov) lists destinations along with their requirements and recommendations for vaccinations. It also lists health departments in the United States that can either assist you or refer you to a travel clinic.

Travel Health Online (www.tripprep.com) has a reputation for having more up-to-date and reliable data regarding immunizations, though it does require that you sign in for the information.

Regardless of my faint-inducing fear of needles (no wonder I never joined the trend of tattoo-wearing hipsters), I faithfully get my immunization updates and visit a travel clinic prior to every journey.

Carry an International Certificate of Vaccination, more commonly called a "yellow health card," issued by your doctor, which includes an official stamp for all immunizations.

9. STAYING HEALTHY ON THE ROAD

You'll need to show this upon entering any country with vaccine requirements.

First-Aid Kit

While you can purchase a packaged first-aid kit, preparing your own is easy. Carry travel-size versions of everything, and consolidate pills such as aspirin into well-marked pill cases.

To prevent being bitten by insects such as mosquitoes, numerous types of flies, bees, ticks, and other annoying creatures, wear long sleeves and pants. ExOfficio (www.exofficio.com) has a clothing line called Buzz Off Insect Shield that includes bug repellant woven into the fabric. In some parts of the world (Alaska and Australia, for instance), you can purchase hats with netting that cover your face or with small corks dangling off the brim to ward off flying bugs. (Apparently you're allowed to look embarrassingly silly when your state or national bird is jokingly considered the mosquito!)

Hot Tip! Pack a pair of flip flops or purchase a pair upon arrival (they're super cheap nearly everywhere you go), and always wear them in the shower to keep any nasty creepy crawlies and fungus off your feet.

Natural Remedies

Prevention may just be the best natural remedy of all. There are a number of simple things you can do to avoid the spread of germs, including washing your hands often; using an antibacterial gel or moist towelettes; opening doors (especially bathrooms) with a paper towel or your sleeve pulled over your hand, or pushing it with your foot or elbow; pushing elevator buttons with your knuckle; and avoiding touching your mouth and eyes with your hands.

Make It Natural

When traveling to Australia a number of years ago, I developed a rash on my arm that began when I scraped it on a park bench with peeling paint. A local pharmacist recommended an antihistamine. Being on a tight budget and not wanting to ingest medicine if I didn't have to, I picked up a bottle of tea tree oil and applied it to the rash over several days. The rash disappeared, with no side effects. Indigenous to Australia, tea tree oil is widely known to be a natural antiseptic, antibacterial, and fungicide. The aboriginals have been using this for thousands of years to solve numerous health issues. It certainly cleared up my rash!—BW

While you may be tempted to take a medication to relieve the symptoms of a minor health problem, a supplement or natural remedy will help eliminate the root cause of the problem while helping you maintain a healthier immune system overall. In addition to a first-aid kit with medicinal products, use natural prophylaxes and remedies to prevent and deal with anything from jet lag to cuts, bruises and rashes.

If you don't already incorporate natural alternatives into your lifestyle, consider the following as a starting point: Avon's Skin So Soft (good for short-term use only) or oil of lemon eucalyptus (for ages 3 and up) as a mosquito repellent, carob powder or blackberry root (from a health-food store) as an antidiarrheal, tiger balm for headaches, No-Jet-Lag (www.nojetlag.com) homeopathic tablets to reduce the effects of jet lag, Airborne (www.airbornehealth.com) tablets as an immune system booster, antibacterial hand gel, antibacterial travel wipes, and tea tree oil or gel for scrapes and cuts.

❦ On the Flight

Following a healthy regimen during your journey will help you arrive relaxed and energized. Here are some ways to stave off jet lag and feel your best for arrival.

❦ Liquids

Flying dehydrates you. Drink a glass of water for every hour of flight and resist the temptation to drink alcohol and coffee (both of which can cause further dehydration). Staying hydrated will help you thwart off airborne illnesses and keep you feeling better overall. If you have a small bladder, consider an aisle seat so you aren't trapped when your seatmate falls asleep.

❦ Eating Healthfully

Long flights can be boring, and the tendency is to eat just to have something to do. Resist the food tray that the airlines provide, and instead take your own healthy snacks, such as fruit, nuts, seeds, or protein bars.

It's better to eat a small bag of healthy snacks (though even just a quarter cup of walnuts has 200 calories) than a thousand calories of fat, grease, sugar, and carbs. Since you'll be stationary for an extended period of time, portion them out so that you're eating a smaller amount than normal.

❦ Exercise

Deep-vein thrombosis (DVT) occurs when a blood clot forms in your leg after long periods of sitting still. It is potentially fatal if fragments of the clot move into your lungs. It kills young and old alike. NBC news reporter David Bloom died in Iraq as a result of DVT due to sitting in an army tank for an extended period of time. To minimize your risk, you can purchase compression socks that reduce swelling and fatigue. Try products from Ames Walker (www.ameswalker.com) or Injinji (www.injinji.com).

While flying, stretch in your seat every hour or two, and take walks up and down the aisle on longer flights. Try the following: rotate your ankles, pump your feet up and down, bring your knees to your chest (one at a time), roll your shoulders and neck, and stretch your shoulders by crossing your arms across your chest one at a time.

Jet Lag

Jet lag is caused by a change in your circadian rhythm, which is essentially a disruption in the amount of light and dark to which you are exposed. When traveling across numerous time zones, your body gets out of sync with the time at your destination and literally becomes confused as to when to eat and sleep. While not usually debilitating, it can be annoying since you will want to maximize the time you spend awake once you arrive.

There are a number of things you can do to help offset jet lag.

No-Jet-Lag is a homeopathic tablet that contains chamomile and is proven to be safe and effective by inducing a light sleep. Order from the company's website or pick it up at your local pharmacy or grocery store.

I don't recommend taking sleeping pills as they can really knock you out. While it may be a good idea to nap, you'll want it to be done lightly enough so that you move around to keep your circulation flowing. Pills could also cause you to arrive drowsy at your destination, making you more of a target for theft or crime.

❧ At Your Destination

Once you arrive, set your watch to the local time and conduct yourself accordingly. If it's the middle of the night, sleep and get rest. Set your alarm for morning so that you can get on track with the local time. Use natural aids such as eye shades, ear plugs, or noise-canceling headphones to help you sleep.

The secret is to not take *the nap*. "It's the nap that will do you in," says Stefany, a landscaper who loves the outdoors. "I took a nap when I arrived in New Zealand, and I was a wreck for three days. Usually, I try to take really boring books so I get sleepy on the plane. I wouldn't take Harry Potter or something that would enthrall me."

❧ Water

It's tempting to drink less-healthy liquids such as soda or juice, as they can often be less expensive than bottled water. However, nothing beats H_2O, and if you can use a refillable container such as one from Sigg, you'll ultimately save some bucks and be kinder to the environment by reusing. If possible, fill up your bottle from the cooler in your hotel lobby or in the gym of your hotel, rather than from the tap. Or use a water purifier such as the SteriPEN (www.steripen.com).

If you're unsure about the quality of water at your hotel, check your guidebook or ask other travelers or the staff whether the water in the country you're visiting is potable.

When tap water is iffy, don't swallow it when showering or bathing, and use bottled water to brush your teeth. Be vigilant.

With bottled water, check that the cap is secure and intact, ensuring that it's not a bottle that has just been refilled from a tap. You might also question where pitchers of "fresh" water actually come from when served at a hotel or restaurant. It upset

Leslie, who is an experienced traveler, to watch a ritual where she was staying. "I once saw the maid at my hotel in Merida, Mexico, filling the water pitcher in my room from a faucet in the courtyard and then placing a fresh linen on top!"

You may not want to give up your morning orange juice, but be aware that when purchasing fruit juices from street vendors, the fruit may be fresh and clean, but the utensils they're using to cut the fruit may not be. And if a street vendor supplies you with a straw, make sure it's new. Oftentimes, these are reused. Yuck.

Hot Tip! Don't share water bottles, utensils, or anything else you'd put in your mouth with anyone but your closest traveling companion.

Health-Conscious Eating

While you're traveling, try new foods, but don't eat more calories than you would at home. Sample a couple of appetizers rather than a full meal or eat five or six snacks throughout the day, rather than three large meals. What could be more fun than picking out fresh items from an open air market, food stall, or bakery as you survey a new city?

Grocery stores can be an experience unto themselves whether in another region of your own country or abroad. They can also be the source of healthy and light snacks. The food will be fresh, you can control your portion sizes, and you'll probably save a dollar or two.

Based on her experience, Elyse says, "eat your big meal at lunch when you're more comfortable by yourself and grab something small for dinner." This advice serves multiple purposes. Lunch-sized portions are cheaper than dinner, it gives you a good chunk of the day to work off the calories, and you'll feel less self-conscious eating lunch by yourself.

Cruises pose a particular challenge because of the large quantity of "free" food available around the clock. While difficult, it's not impossible to eat healthily and lightly. Consider going vegetarian to inhibit yourself from eating large portions of steak and chicken. Or begin every meal with a green salad so that you fill up on that, rather than on a loaf of bread. In addition, regularly visit the on-board gym, swim, dance, and walk at every opportunity.

In cafés, flatware is often kept at a central location, and chopsticks are often found in a holder on the table—both places where customers freely breathe, sneeze, and wheeze. If you're eating at a restaurant where the utensils are kept in a public place for all to paw through, give them a quick wash-down with an alcohol wipe and a clean napkin prior to eating.

If you have special dietary requirements (vegetarian or vegan, for instance) you may have to allow for some flexibility. You risk offending your hosts if you arrive in a tiny village where they have slaughtered their weekly chicken in your honor. I should know. I've done it myself. I must have appeared like a freak in an indigenous Vietnamese Montagnard community when I turned down both their chicken meal and homemade wine so I could stick to my self-imposed eating habits. I regret it now, and today would be honored if I had the chance to experience it all over.

❧ Exercise

If you have an exercise routine at home, stick to it as much as possible. If your accommodation doesn't have a gym, you can stretch, practice yoga, do push-ups and sit-ups, or go for a jog.

Athletic-Minded Traveler (www.athleticmindedtraveler.com) lists health-conscious restaurants, workout locations, and jogging routes for North American cities.

When booking a room for business travel, I always make sure that my hotel has a gym or workout area. My business trips are generally short, and I don't have time for the long walks that I take at home. A Stairmaster or treadmill allow me to spend a solid 30 to 45 minutes on a good aerobic workout.

Take as many opportunities as possible to walk when you sightsee or are heading out to eat. These small jaunts add up, and can really help keep off the pounds.

❀ Female Health Issues

As a woman, you may encounter specific issues that men don't worry about. Being prepared can help you evade a minor nuisance or, potentially, a more serious illness.

❀ Menstruation

You might miss your period completely for months while you're on the road, or you may get it at a time when you're not expecting it. This can be caused by stress, heat, or as a result of being out of your daily routine. There's no need to worry unless this goes on for an unusually extended period of time or if there's a possibility that you may be pregnant.

If the situation continues, ask your embassy for a recommendation and visit a doctor's office in a city or town with up-to-date testing capabilities and equipment. If you suspect you have a serious problem, consider returning home to address potential issues.

Tampons and sanitary pads are not readily available in all countries. Action for Southern Africa (www.actsa.org) has a campaign called "Dignity. Period!" to help provide basic sanitary products for the women of Zimbabwe, where they are considered a luxury item. While this is an extreme example, prepare yourself for the worst. Pack what you think you'll need for the whole trip, or at least enough to get you to where you are confident you can purchase more.

While packing small OB tampons can save space in your luggage, if you're going to be in developing countries or remote areas you may want to take tampons with applicators, as you can cleanly insert these. Carry moist towelettes in case there's no way to wash up.

You can do away with tampons and pads by using the DivaCup (www.divacup.com). Made of a soft, medical-grade silicone, the DivaCup collects menstrual flow. It only needs to be emptied two or three times in a 24-hour period, and it can be worn up to 12 hours at a time. Safe and easy to use, this is the ideal travel companion.

Hot Tip! Consider taking a hiatus from your period altogether by taking "the pill" continuously (i.e., skipping the placebo pills). This is not recommended for more than three months, but it's an excellent way to avoid dealing with your monthly cycle while traveling.

Contraception

If you are on the pill, your period should continue to be regular throughout your travels, and you won't need to worry about getting pregnant. Take enough for the entire trip, and note that antibiotics can render the pill ineffective.

If there is the slightest possibility that you will be having sex, use a condom. The pill will not give you protection against sexually transmitted diseases. And do not be shy about asking your sexual partner to use them. An STD is the last souvenir you want to bring home.

Yeast Infection

Yeast infections are caused by stress, antibiotics, tight clothing, or even wearing a bathing suit for an extended period of time. If you think you have a yeast infection, which is accompanied by itching, discharge, burning during urination, rash, and odor, apply an over-the-counter vaginal cream, eat yogurt with acidophilus, or see a doctor for a prescription if symptoms persist for more than a week. If you're prone to yeast infections, consider taking your usual medications along with you.

Bladder Infection

Symptoms include burning while urinating, frequent urination, and dark-colored urine. A mild case of this will clear up in a few days on its own, but drinking lots of water and/or cranberry juice will help.

Pregnancy

If you must travel for work or would like one last trip before giving birth, the second trimester is the best time for scheduling a trip. The worst nausea will be over in the first three months, the risk of a premature delivery will be low in the second trimester, and you may be extremely uncomfortable during your final months.

Airline policies differ, but some forbid travel in the last month of pregnancy on domestic flights and during the last five weeks on international flights. Bulkhead seats will give you more leg room, but you'll have to place all carry-on bags in the overhead compartment, making it difficult for you to get to your things.

Options for where you can travel will also be limited, as many vaccinations and medications required for entry into a country are either unsafe or untested for pregnant women. If you become infected with a disease such as malaria, it can severely affect your unborn child. Consult with your doctor before making plans, to avoid potential hazards or problems.

⚘ Managing an Illness or Injury

If you are in a developing country, go to a doctor or hospital that is known for treating foreigners. While some medical professionals in developing countries have been trained abroad or have been educated in the importance of hygiene, many do not have this same level of education. In poorer areas, it's likely that the overall health care system is outdated and the latest methods of cleanliness are not in place.

The International Association of Medical Assistance to Travellers (www.iamat.org) is a nonprofit organization that can refer you to English-speaking, Western-trained doctors. In addition, they advise travelers on health risks and immunization requirements, as well as the sanitary conditions of water, milk, and food around the world.

If you do not have a life-threatening condition, don't dismiss doctors who practice age-old medicine such as ayurvedic (practiced in India for thousands of years) or herbal treatments. These won't mend your broken arm, but you could get rid of that nasty cold or stomach flu by relying on the wisdom of these highly trained (and often inexpensive) practitioners.

In the tropics, keep a close watch on any skin problems such as bug bites, scratches, and skin irritations. It's easy for these to become infected due to dirty ocean, pool, river, or tap water. To avoid infections, keep these covered with a bandage or simply stay out of the water.

The upside to getting ill in another country is that it will provide you with an opportunity to experience the hospitality of the locals. When Sarah was trekking on the Annapurna loop in Nepal, she got giardia from dirty drinking water. She was forced to abandon the trek, and returned to her starting point in Pokara, where the proprietor of her guest house watched over her and helped her through the illness for two weeks. "The proprietor was nicer to me than the traveling companions I had been trekking with!"

✿ Health Issues You May Encounter

There are a number of health-related issues to be aware of while you're traveling. What may seem like a slight annoyance at home could become more of an issue when you're traveling. A simple scratch on your skin, for example, could become infected in tropical climates, and exposure to intense sun could give you a nasty burn if you're not careful. Exotic illnesses such as amoebic dysentery or yellow fever may never have crossed your radar prior to planning a trip but could be quite common at your destination.

As a solo traveler, you'll want to be especially aware if a health-related issue affects you, as you'll be the only one looking out for yourself and your best interests.

Always consult a doctor who's well-versed on travel vaccinations prior to your departure, or consult the websites listed in this chapter's Immunizations section for more information.

Sunburn—Melanomas caused by the depletion of the ozone layer (there's actually a hole in the ozone hovering over the southern hemisphere) can be thwarted by wearing sunscreen and sun-protective clothing, including a hat, and staying out of the sun. Even short periods of time spent under cloudy skies in the tropics can cause sunburn.

Travelers' Diarrhea—According to the CDC, travelers' diarrhea (commonly called Delhi Belly or Montezuma's Revenge, depending on where you're traveling) is the most common illness affecting travelers. It's caused by bacteria in unhygienic food and water. In addition to watery bowel movements, symptoms can include nausea, vomiting, abdominal cramping, and fever.

Amoebic Dysentery—Here's a fascinating piece of info: Amoebas usually die in your stomach when you've ingested contaminated food or water, and therefore cause few side effects (stomach cramps, diarrhea). However, when these little critters turn into cysts by building a wall around themselves and are then passed to humans due to unsanitary conditions (in feces or an individual not properly washing their hands), it can be quite harmful. While amoebic dysentery is rare in travelers, the main symptom is bloody diarrhea. Complications of the liver can occur if it's left untreated. Avoid contaminated water and food by following the old adage: Cook it, peel it, boil it, or forget it. Also avoid direct contact with individuals in unclean environments.

Insect Bites, Scratches or Skin Rashes—Even the most innocuous insect bite can turn into an inflamed nuisance if not properly taken care of, especially in tropical areas. Keep any breaks in your skin clean and far from water of dubious quality. (This includes a dirty ocean.) Immediately use an antibacterial topical cream to prevent infection, and lessen itching by using an anti-itch cream.

Giardia—Caused by parasites in your gastrointestinal tract, symptoms can be really unpleasant. (I know from experience!)

Bloating, severe gas, and diarrhea all accompany giardia. Avoid dirty water and food. If you do end up with a severe case of the trots caused by giardia, there are a couple of (also) unpleasant treatments. The drugs Flagyl, Furoxone, Tinidazole, and Quinacrine can all be used for treating the illness. Local pharmacies where you're traveling may even carry these as over-the-counter drugs. While these are all considered to be highly effective (and really the only way to get rid of giardia completely), the side effects can include nausea and a metallic taste in your mouth.

Malaria—Transmitted through mosquitoes, malaria is potentially life-threatening if not treated. Before going on a trip, consult a doctor at a travel clinic or one that specializes in travel health regarding advice on your destination. There is a lot of controversy over the effectiveness of some preventive medications, due to their severe side effects. Avoid being bitten in the first place by using insect repellent, wearing long sleeves and long pants (preferably with an insect repellent built in), use a mosquito net, and burn mosquito coils.

Hepatitis—There are various strains of the hepatitis virus. Vaccinations are available for hepatitis A (caused by contaminated food and water) and B (transmitted through sex). Hepatitis C (transmitted through blood, such as transfusions) and E (contaminated water and food) do not have vaccines. Get vaccinated for A and B, avoid a transfusion if there's no ability to screen for hepatitis C, and make sure your food is safe for consumption.

Tetanus and Diphtheria—Booster shots are needed every 10 years. These will prevent infections caused by an open cut (tetanus) and upper-respiratory infections (diphtheria) caused by bacteria.

Dengue Fever—Another mosquito-borne illness, dengue fever has become increasingly prevalent in the tropics. Symptoms can be more severe than malaria, and can include high fever, headache and body aches, as well as a rash and diarrhea. There is no treatment or prophylaxis.

Japanese Encephalitis—Transmitted by mosquitoes, this viral infection is found primarily in Southeast Asia. It causes headaches and fever and, as it progresses, convulsions and potentially coma. While it is rare for travelers to become infected, those staying in rural areas for more than a month should be vaccinated, as one-third of those infected die.

Yellow Fever—Yellow fever, spread by mosquitoes, is accompanied by fever and a jaundiced appearance. It's found mostly in Africa and South America. Vaccinations are required for entry into some countries, while they are only recommended for others.

HIV—The virus that causes AIDS is spread through contaminated body fluids. You should never, ever have unprotected sex or come in contact with a needle that has not been sterilized, including those at tattoo parlors and medical facilities. The rate of HIV/AIDS infection is growing rapidly, particularly in Africa, Asia, and India.

⚜ Potty Talk

You may be surprised to find that many toilets around the world are nothing more than a hole in the ground with a couple of ceramic "footings" on either side so you don't slip. In remote areas and in developing countries, you may be lucky to find even that much luxury. Here's one section where I'll leave out the anecdotes!

Suffice it to say that you should be prepared to encounter anything, and take your own roll of toilet paper (found in major cities, even in places where it's rarely used). In countries such as India, TP is rarely an option; that's where your left hand comes in so handy.

And if you're actually using a flush toilet, the world's sewage systems rarely can handle toilet paper as well as those in North America. You may notice a small garbage can next to the toilet. If there's no sign warning you not to flush your TP, take that little bucket as a signal to use it for your paper products.

On long bus rides when you may be stopping in remote areas to use the "loo" (as the British say), you may want to cut back on what you eat and drink so that you can avoid using a makeshift outhouse, toilet, bathroom, restroom, or hole. I'm not a proponent of using drugs, but an antidiarrheal can come in super handy under these circumstances.

Always carry an antibacterial hand gel in case you encounter the above situations.

10.

PACK IT UP

THERE'S *a fine line between having enough to wear and packing light. The more varied the activities you'll be participating in, the more difficult it will be to pare down. Except in very rare cases, I travel with only carry-on luggage. I wear basic colors, tops, and pants that can be cross-coordinated, and I accessorize for variety.*

✿ Packing List

Creating a packing list will ensure that you don't overlook anything important and will help you get organized. I keep a standard list on my computer that I print out in advance of each trip so I'm not starting from scratch each time.

Track the weather at your destination with the Weather Channel (www.weather.com) and, though it's hard to imagine what 85 degrees feels like if you're in snowy Minneapolis, pack according to the conditions you'll encounter.

On rare occasions, I've ended up with a couple of things I never wear (an extra pair of jeans or a shirt) or lack one or two items. (I forgot to pack a tank top for Costa Rica!) If you've forgotten anything other than your passport and money, you can always purchase it on the road.

Betty Ann suggests buying an item or two of local clothing during your trip. "I found myself in the desert of Timbuktu, and all I had were shorts and a tank top, which were completely inappropriate. I bought a royal Malian head-to-toe robe as soon as I arrived, and wore it the first day. It was a hit with my tour group and with the locals."

Hot Tip! Take a pair of pants that convert to shorts with you when traveling to climates with wide temperature swings or when you'll need pants for an evening out but the days are warm. A hidden zipper around your thigh allows you to unzip the bottom portion so that you can instantly have shorts.

✿ Clothes

Start the packing process at least a week before your departure. Don't wait until the last minute to find out that your shorts no longer fit since you've been dieting or that your favorite shirt got stained when you spilled Italian wine on it while studying maps of Tuscany.

Begin by packing a few basic items in dark colors (unless you're going to a scorching-hot destination). Be prepared to wear the same clothes a number of times. There's no need to feel self-conscious about repeats in your travel clothes. It's unlikely that anyone will notice or care. Your back will thank you for having reduced the weight of your luggage, and you'll be more agile because you'll be carrying fewer items. Alandra, a high-tech project manager who loves to travel, advises, "Be able to carry your own stuff. I don't want to be burdened with the safety issues of carrying too much."

TravelSmith (www.travelsmith.com) specializes in travel clothing, including wrinkle-free attire. Travel clothes from ExOfficio are also wrinkle free, easy to wash and quick to dry. Outdoor-gear stores such as Recreational Equipment, Inc. (www.rei.com) also carry a full line of clothing designed for travel (and sporting) comfort, including Columbia Sportswear Company (www.columbia.com). Several companies, including ExOfficio and Coolibar (www.coolibar.com), offer sun-protective clothing.

If you think you'll be out on the town at some point, pack a dress or skirt and blouse. Bring shoes that can be used for various occasions (sandals that can be worn with a dress or as walking shoes, for instance).

Hot Tip! Bring black underwear so you don't have to worry about bleaching it, or carry disposable OneDerWear (www.onederwear. com), which you can wash out and use several times before throwing them away.

10. PACK IT UP

Pack clothing that is appropriate and respectful of the culture at your destination so that you won't feel uncomfortable or stick out like a tourist. To avoid wearing a sign that says, "I'm a North American," steer clear of logo T-shirts, white sneakers, baseball caps, flip-flops, and tank tops (unless you're at the beach). When in socially conservative countries, make sure that anything that should be covered up is covered up (elbows, knees, etc.).

On a six-month backpacking trip through Asia, I dressed like a backpacker. While I was comfortable, I was treated like, well, a backpacker. My bags were routinely searched by security staff at the airports, and the locals had less regard for me. In contrast, the locals, while poorer than I, took greater care in how they dressed and presented themselves.

Rather than packing bulkier items that take up a lot of space in your luggage, such as a jacket, wear them on the plane. Since the air in a plane can go from drafty to warm in a moment, if you dress in layers, you'll be more comfortable. And you'll be able to reserve space for souvenirs on the return trip. Be sure to set out on your adventure in shoes and clothes that fit well and are broken in.

Packing cubes are an excellent way to organize your items. These are soft-sided cubes that you pack clothes, accessories, and other items into and allow easy access without pulling everything out of your luggage. You can then slide breakables between the cubes.

Compression bags are another great alternative. They are sturdy plastic bags with a zip-style closure that allow you to squeeze the air out of your clothes, making a brick-like stack that maximizes space. These can be found at outdoor stores and container stores. Eagle Creek (www.eaglecreek.com)

makes a very reliable version. If you use these, keep a few pieces of clothing out of the bag in which to wrap delicate items, such as a camera.

If your trip is longer than a week, plan to do laundry while you're away. You can wash light cotton clothing in your hotel-room sink and hang it to dry in your room or on the balcony if you have one. Inquire with your hotel whether they have laundry service, or ask for the nearest Laundromat. This just might be a great way to meet some locals, too!

Hot Tip! When you arrive in your room, confirm that the iron and ironing board are in good condition, without any goo on them. If you don't check, once heated up, that goo is going to become part of your wardrobe.

⚘ Toiletries

Transfer your favorite shampoo, conditioner, soaps, and lotions into 3-ounce travel-size bottles. I seal my bottles with shipping tape so they don't leak. This type of tape is usually strong enough to withstand getting somewhat wet from your shower, but don't let it get soaked, or it'll lose its stickiness. Alternately, put a piece of plastic wrap under the lid to prevent spills. Carry small samples of perfume if you wear a fragrance. Pack medications and, if current airport security measures allow, basic toiletries in your carry-on, in case your luggage gets lost.

If you're staying in at least a mid-priced hotel, your room will often include amenities such as shampoo, conditioner, and a hair dryer. If you have any doubt the hotel supplies these items, check in advance so you have fewer things to pack.

Hot Tip! Kiss-Off (www.kissoff.com) is a lip-balm-sized stain remover in a tube that you can easily carry with you. This non-toxic stick can remove lipstick, blood, wine, and coffee, among many other stains, and only needs to be mixed with water to work effectively.

❧ Accessories

Accessorize with simple jewelry and a scarf. Each time you change your accessories, you'll feel as though you're wearing a new outfit.

Leave the bling at home. The easiest way to call attention to yourself is by wearing expensive jewels. Even "fake" jewels that look expensive can be an invitation for someone to snatch your purse or backpack, or pull a necklace off of your neck.

❧ Creature Comforts

You might have a special food item, or perhaps tea or coffee that you can't live without. Why not bring it? A favorite clothing item may make you feel at home away from home.

While trekking through Nepal on my first international adventure, I met a group of Israelis high up in the mountains who were brewing their much-loved coffee from home. I was astounded that they would "waste" precious space in their backpack for what I considered a luxury item. Now, I never leave home without my favorite tea bags, and fondly think back to the Israelis' foresight to carry their creature comforts with them.

Randy Mackenzie is co-owner of Edwards Luggage (www. edwardsluggage.com) in San Francisco. She couldn't agree more. "Bring your little luxuries, whether it's a down travel pillow or blanket, a small candle or eye mask." These items can be found at your local travel clothing and accessory store or online.

Be sure to take a new journal, and treat yourself to new pens, paints, or pencils to help you document your journey.

Camera

Unless you're a professional and need to carry lots of gear, plan to take the smallest camera possible for the types of images you plan to be shooting. Not only are small cameras ideal for packing, as they take up less space, it's easier to whip out a hand-sized digital for quick snaps of the rumbling volcano before you run.

If your camera has a built-in battery, don't forget the docking station or power cord. It could be very difficult to find a compatible one while on the road.

MP3 Player

On a crowded bus while traveling from Mexico City to Guatemala, I felt completely over stimulated. I found that being able to tune into some of my favorite music on my MP3 player not only helped me to pass the time on the long ride, it also allowed me to tune out the women modestly throwing up into small bags from motion sickness while kids were screaming around me.

Used sparingly, I advocate MP3 players as a way to relax and be transported to another place and time if you need some down time. Conversely, an MP3 player can help you become immersed in your foreign environment if you create a special play list for the location before your trip. Just keep in mind that while MP3 players are ubiquitous in North America, they could be considered rude by some cultures, as you block out the surrounding environment.

Hot Tip! Rather than carrying books, consider downloading an audio book or two that pertains to your destination. Audible (www. audible.com) and iTunes (www.apple.com /itunes) are excellent re-sources for downloadable books.

Some MP3 players come with audio- and video-recording de-vices, or have adaptors for such purposes. With an MP3 player, you can capture a marimba band at Carnival or the frantic rhythm of a punk band in Amsterdam, and share them when you return home.

Photo-storage devices are built into a many brands of MP3 players. I upload photos from home onto my iPod and share them with people I meet during my journeys.

Electricity—Electrical outlets in most foreign countries will require a different prong configuration than what your elec-tronic equipment uses at home. Bring a universal converter package, which you can pick up at any travel store or on-line at Magellan's Travel Supplies (www.magellans.com). Requirements vary by country; consequently, double check that you're buying the correct one for your destination.

Hot Tip! When packing electronics (camera, MP3 player, etc.), place the on /off switch in the "lock" position so the batteries won't drain if the device accidentally gets switched on. If the device doesn't have a "lock" position, but it holds standard batteries, you can flip the batter-ies around.

Be sure to carry extra batteries if your electronic device doesn't have one that is built-in.

♣ Noise-canceling Headphones

Expensive? Yes. Priceless? You bet. These battery-operated headphones reduce extraneous noise, effectively eliminating background noise on trains, planes, and buses. You can wear them without plugging them into a listening device or, as with any set of headphones, you can connect them to your MP3 player or DVD player, or into the headphone jack of an airplane. The first time I tried a pair of these I was amazed at just how much background noise there is on a plane, which I had never noticed before.

Bose (www.bose.com) is one of the best brands on the market. Bose QuietComfort 3 Acoustic Noise Cancelling headphones retail for about $350 and can be purchased online or at a kiosk located in most major airports throughout North America.

♣ Gifts

Traveling companions and locals alike will be appreciative if you leave them with a small, inexpensive gift. When traveling to developing countries, I shop at my local dollar store to stock up on items to share. I buy key chains that include a picture of local sights (the Space Needle and Mount Rainier), and candy, wind-up toys, beaded bracelets, and pencils for children.

For more-developed regions, I bring a few nicer items from the Pacific Northwest, including locally made chocolates or small bags of coffee.

Postcards from your home city can help to break down barriers and start conversations with taxi drivers and ice-cream vendors alike.

🐾🐾🐾 Alison's Story 🐾🐾🐾

When I fly in to a location to go camping, I carry my tent, sleeping bag (which I cram into a compression stuff sack), stove, cook set, headlamp (with extra batteries), maps, GPS, granola bars, hiking boots, and clothes.

Airlines don't allow you to carry on or check fuel onto a plane, so I buy it at my destination, as well as enough food to get me through the trip, or at least until I get to a place where I can purchase more food. I buy nonperishable items, or foods that won't go bad quickly. This includes dry soups, nuts, cereals, and string cheese. I check on the Internet before departing for sporting-goods or camping stores at my destination, and make sure that the fuel they carry is compatible with my stove.

If I'm carrying ice axes or climbing hardware, I cover the adze and pick, and wrap them well inside my backpack so that they don't slice anything. Most airlines will provide you with a sturdy plastic bag to wrap your backpack in. This protects your outside straps, and makes it easier for the baggage handlers. I recommend these bags for anytime that you don't have direct control over your bag (like in a bus or train).

I keep the amount of clothing I pack to a minimum, and then wash my clothes at a Laundromat along the way or rinse them out in a sink where I'm staying. Lightweight, wrinkle-free clothes will dry out overnight. This is not only for convenience, but as a matter of safety in the mountains, where wet clothes can be dangerous. On a typical 10-day trip, my pack will weigh about 55 pounds. This includes 12 pounds of food, as well as climbing gear. If I am simply backpacking (and not climbing), the weight comes to about 35 pounds, including food.

Take an extra bag (that's lightweight and compact) or plan to buy one for souvenirs. I now fondly use the "Paris" duffel bag that I bought on the last day of my trip to France to carry home all of my trip purchases. Try to buy these extra goodies in the last day or two of your trip.

☙ Camping Gear

Packing up your camping gear requires special attention for women traveling solo. To ensure you're not encumbered with lots of stuff, pack the smallest and lightest versions of everything you'll need, including backpack, tent, and sleeping bag. You'll be saving some dough by not staying in hotels, so outfit yourself with high-quality, easy-to-carry gear. Otherwise, you risk exhaustion from hauling around more pounds than you can handle.

If you take only what you'll need, and leave the pillow, extra pans and inflatable sleeping pad at home, your pack will be lighter, too. And, if you need to get out of a sticky situation quickly, you'll have less baggage to handle.

☙ Gear for Special Hobbies

The biggest obstacle with traveling to pursue your favorite hobby, whether scuba diving, golfing, surfing, skiing, playing music, or snowboarding, will be safely getting your gear from one place to another. Whenever possible, rent gear at your destination.

If you do choose to bring equipment with you, carry on smaller items, such as snorkel gear, and check bulkier items in well-packed duffel bags or cases made especially for your sport or hobby. While you will still be restricted by your airline's rules for carry-on items, you can usually board with delicate items such as guitars. (One airline representative admitted to me that whether you are able to carry one of these larger items on board is often at the whim of the flight attendants and staff.)

Expect to be charged by the airlines for additional bags beyond their posted limits and for overweight bags.

When you check in, I suggest paying a skycap at the curbside check-in the small additional fee to take your bags. It will help you (and other passengers) stay more relaxed since you won't be stumbling over gear while checking in.

Types of Luggage

You'll need to determine which type of luggage to use based on the type of travel you're planning. Business, casual, and adventure travelers will each have different needs. Debra, a manufacturer's representative in the luggage industry, has lots of experience in this area. "If you are a frequent business or adventure traveler, you will want something that holds up. But if you're traveling to Grandma's once a year, you don't need anything expensive."

Debra has noticed a number of changes over the years. "After 9/11, airlines started enforcing their weight limits, to increase revenue. They now charge for luggage that's over 50 pounds for domestic flights. The luggage industry began creating lighter luggage in response. Around the same time, manufacturers began creating bags that appeal to women through color and design, and they are doing some fun things with fabrics."

Hot Tip! Attach a ribbon or bright luggage tag to your bag so it stands out, whether on a baggage carousel or on a bus filled with backpacks, gear, and produce.

Business Travel—A garment bag is the best choice for packing dress clothes and evening wear. Bags are available as bi- or tri-folds, and some can fold up small enough to slip under the airplane seat in front of you.

Unless you want to purchase several sizes of luggage, base your choice on how much room you'll need for the average length of trips you plan to take. As always, pack as little as possible.

Choose a bag with a variety of pockets located outside and inside, and utilize these for your underwear and other smaller items. Wear your heaviest shoes and pack additional ones away. You're probably carrying your most expensive outfits, so purchase a high-quality bag that won't easily rip or tear.

While you may not be able to eliminate all creases and wrinkles, using plastic dry-cleaning bags between each layer of clothing can help cut down on wrinkles when the bag is folded and stored on the plane.

Casual Travel—Soft-sided (or duffel) bags and semi-soft cases are great for the casual or weekend traveler. Soft-sided bags are lightweight and easy to stow in overhead bins or toss in the trunk of a car. A semi-soft case (covered in fabric, but with a frame inside) will provide your items with a little more protection from wrinkles and crushing, and it often has internal pockets for shoes, paperwork, and other items.

Adventure Travel—Within this category, there are a couple of options for backpacks:

Travel Packs—These generally come in one size, which can be adjusted using hip and shoulder straps. They open like a suitcase for ease in packing. They may have wheels or come with a daypack that zips off. According to Lauren, a travel-pack specialist at REI, "Women-specific travel packs are a growing market. These packs are based on women having narrower shoulders and waists, as well as shorter torsos."

She suggests a wheeled travel pack, "for women who don't want a backpack but who may need to carry their bag up stairs or over cobblestone streets in Europe."

Wilderness Packs—These internal-frame packs are made for long-term outdoor trips. They provide excellent support and are more comfortable than travel packs when carrying lots of gear. They are a little harder to pack and unpack, as they load vertically, but they balance better on your back.

The key for choosing any bag is that the bag be person-specific. What fits one woman may not fit another well at all. Test out various types with weight in the bag to determine the comfort level. If you live in a remote region, REI's website has in-depth information on choosing the best pack for your type of travel and torso size.

Amy, who spent half a year in India, suggests that if you do travel with a backpack, people will instantly see you differently. "I would leave my backpack in the taxi when I arrived at my hotel and tell the driver that I would be right back to go shopping, to ensure he would stay there. I would then check into the hotel and go back to the taxi to get the backpack, or actually have the driver take me shopping." She felt the hotel clerks treated her better if they didn't see her backpack.

This perception is common in Europe. Even though Mary had first-class train tickets, when they saw her backpack, "The businessmen were indignant. I would be asked to move from my reserved seat for them. I would apologize up and down but still insist that I keep my seat."

Hot Tip! If you're checking luggage, be sure that it is properly tagged for your destination. I have caught baggage attendants putting the wrong destination tag on my bags a half-dozen times. It only has to happen once before you learn to watch where your bag is going!

Carry-on Luggage

Check with your airline for any travel restrictions for carry-on luggage and, whenever possible, bring a daypack that includes a day's worth of necessities. Susan Foster, author of *Smart Packing for Today's Travelers*, suggests "carrying an extra shirt so that you have one to wear later and one that can be washed" if your checked luggage gets lost.

Daypack—The right daypack is indispensable. It needs to be small enough to slip under the airplane seat in front of you, yet large enough to carry everything you need for a day trip. A bag that is worn across your body, such as a shoulder bag or messenger bag, is more desirable than a purse or small daypack, as they are less easily accessed by thieves and are easier for you to get to than a pack worn on your back. Randy, from Edwards Luggage, recommends the company Pacsafe (www.pacsafe.com) for daypacks. "Their bags have compartments on the inside, are made of microfibers (making them quite soft), are worn flat to the body, and come in many colors." In addition, they are slash-proof and can be worn as a shoulder bag or hip pack.

Maricris was comfortable with using a shoulder bag, as opposed to a backpack, during her weekend jaunts in Europe. "All I needed was a bag that was big enough to fit my travel book, map, small wallet, passport, cell phone, and water bottle. The key feature for me was to have an outside pocket where I could easily stash a map since I was always looking at it."

Luggage Security

The Transportation Security Administration (www.tsa.gov) provides a list of items that are prohibited, regardless of whether they are in your carry-on luggage or your checked bag.

You'll want to keep your bags safe by using a TSA-approved lock. These locks allow security people at the airport to open luggage with the use of specially designed tools. Otherwise, you risk having your locks cut off if security needs to open your bag.

Travel Sentry (www.travelsentry.org) is the facilitator between travel-accessory manufacturers and the TSA. Their locks range in price from about $10 to $20; they can be found online and at travel stores, pharmacies, and department stores.

By using one of these to lock your zippers together, you can prevent the contents from accidentally spilling out, as well as stop a casual thief from opening the bag and sorting through the contents.

Hot Tip! Attach a spare tag to your luggage and include the address of the hotel where you're staying. If your bag gets lost or misplaced, it can be delivered to the hotel at your destination city.

Packing Lists

These three packing lists are my starting point for every trip. But, I don't carry everything listed here for each trip I take! My goodness, if I packed all this, I'd have a heavier pack than Alison. I adjust the quantity and type of clothing articles and accessories based on the season where I'm going, how long the flight is (I carry eyeshades and a pillow for long flights), and the length and purpose of the trip.

Clothes

Jeans	Dress blouses	Socks
Slacks	Suit jacket	Bathing suit
Shorts	Sweater	Gym clothes (top,
Convertible pants /	Light outdoor jacket	shorts, sneakers, socks)
shorts with zip-	or windbreaker	Walking shoes
off legs	Pajamas	Walking / hiking sandals
Casual tops	Underwear	Dress shoes
Tank tops	Bras	Belt

Toiletries

Shampoo	Deodorant	Medications
Conditioner	Cotton swabs	Feminine products
Soap	Facial lotion	Birth control / condoms
Antibacterial gel	Hand lotion	Makeup
Antibacterial wipes	Sunscreen	Bug repellant
Toothbrush	Lip balm	Tissues
Toothpaste	Lipstick	Razor
Dental floss	Hairbrush	
Vitamins	Hair accessories	

Accessories and Documents

Passport	Camera (and charger)
Magazines	Journal and pens
Credit cards	MP3 player (and charger)
Electricity converter	Earplugs
Driver's license	Binoculars
Sleep sack	Inflatable pillow (for long trips)
Snacks	Small spiral notebook (for expenses)
Frequent-flier card	Flashlight (and batteries)
Watch	Cell phone (and charger)
Maps/directions	Travel alarm clock
Business cards	Sunglasses
Phrase book	Eye shades
Books	Microlight (small keychain-sized flashlight)
Digital book reader	Video camera (and charger)

For Business:

Briefcase

Laptop (and power cord)

11.

GADGETS AND GIZMOS

YOU *may want to have instant access to travel information, listen to audio programs pertinent to your destination, or receive travel-related email alerts. You can utilize this information from home, or you can become a flashpacker (one who carries their electronic gear while traveling). While immersing yourself too much in high-tech gear can remove you from the total travel experience, taking advantage of their benefits in a limited capacity can actually help make your journey easier.*

❀ Laptops

For longer trips or if you're traveling with a backpack, it doesn't make sense to lug a laptop around since they are heavy, bulky, and delicate. Internet service is ubiquitous, allowing you to check your email remotely without the hassle of traveling with a laptop.

However, for business travel and shorter trips, you may choose to take your laptop with you to have easy access to the Internet and your work. Free Wi-Fi spots can be found all over the world. I take advantage of these when I'm traveling, just to get out of my hotel room for the evening or day. Wi-Fi-FreeSpot (www.wififreespot.com) lists hotspots in airports, hotels, resorts, restaurants, RV parks, malls, and vacation rentals. You can search by location type (i.e. airport), by state, or by country. By the way, to take advantage of free Wi-Fi, your laptop will need a built-in Wi-Fi receptor or a Wi-Fi card adaptor.

Be sure to secure your laptop from hackers and lookiloos while you're on open Wi-Fi networks by using personal firewall software. You can research the best-available options on CNET Networks (www.cnet.com), which rates top technology products and software.

On flights, getting a window seat will cut down on the number of eyeballs landing on your screen. I sit at a window seat on the right side of the plane, then turn my laptop slightly to the right so that, hopefully, those sitting behind me can't peek between the seats to see my highly secretive documents.

In most rows, the person in front can push his or her seat back, forcing you to fold down your screen. If you sit in a bulkhead seat or in an exit row, you'll have a little extra room to open up the laptop.

Be aware of how long your battery will last, and ensure it's fully powered before you depart your home or hotel. Electrical outlets at the airport are a hot commodity, and you may not be able to power up before or between flights.

Hot Tip! Carry your own multiprong power plug so that you can share power with other travelers at the airport or elsewhere.

While moving through security, don't let other travelers make you feel rushed, which is when accidents can happen. You will be required to remove your laptop from your bag and have it screened separately. Keep an eye on security folks to make sure they are handling it properly. They do a pretty good job but, ultimately, they aren't as concerned about your possessions as you are.

Photography

Whether or not you're a professional photographer, you'll most likely carry a camera with you when traveling. The Travel Photographers Network (www.travelphotographers.net) is filled with inspirational photos and articles to get your creative juices flowing. Photography is well suited for solo travelers since you can set your own schedule. You can get up early for the best light, and move stealthily through markets and the jungle without being hindered by a traveling partner who doesn't share your passion. And photography is particularly well suited for gals, as we can more easily get to know the local women, who may be happy to talk about themselves and their families, and show the female guests around or pose for photos.

Regardless of whether I'm traveling for business, adventure, or relaxation, I always carry a camera with me. You never know what interesting sights or opportunities will present themselves, and you won't want to get caught without the chance to document them. Many years ago, during a July business trip to Rome, I was carrying a backpack filled with camera gear and film. Temperatures were in the 90s, and I was hot and uncomfortable lugging around so much extra weight in the heat. I was uninspired to shoot, even as I took in the Trevi Fountain and the Coliseum. That pretty much cured me of shooting slides. Shortly thereafter, I went digital and now carry about one-eighth the weight of photography-related items I used to.

With digital gear, you can delete photos you don't want, and once you're home, upload your images into an online photo system such as Kodak Gallery (www.kodakgallery.com), Flickr, or Snapfish (www.snapfish.com), so you can share them with friends and family.

While you're on the road, you may be able to upload photos to one of these sites using a USB cable. I wouldn't recommend it as a method of storing your photos in order to delete them from your camera, however, since you won't have the security of having the original version on your own computer's hard drive. Be sure to take along extra memory cards, too.

To prepare myself for the best picture-taking opportunities, I study both how-to books on photography and coffee-table photo books for the area I'm visiting. Photography classes have also helped me fine tune my skills. Community centers and local colleges often have evening and weekend classes taught by experienced photographers. Or you can take a photography tour conducted by a professional.

Before snapping pictures of individuals or important religious or cultural locales, learn whether it's appropriate to do so.

Brenda Tharp's (www.brendatharp.com) photography tours focus on nature, travel, and the outdoors. Her wide range of tours include the California Redwoods and Bhutan. Brenda knows how important it is to study up on the culture before you go. "Photographers who are comfortable shooting people think they can just walk up and start photographing in any culture. That can be an affront to many."

GPS

What exactly is a Global Positioning System (GPS) and how does it work? Glad you asked. Satellites that circle the globe gather positioning information and transmit it back to Earth. GPS receivers take that information and, using precise calculations, display the user's position on the ground with an accuracy of about six to 20 feet, depending on the quality of the unit.

The satellites rely on a direct line of sight with a GPS receiver, so coverage is spotty in areas with a dense forest or inside caves. Alison, a mountain climber and back-country enthusiast, cautions, "You can't completely rely on a GPS, so always carry a map and compass with you." Still, Alison gets plenty of usage from her unit. "I always take my GPS whenever I go to a place I've never been before. It tracks me as I go and allows me to set waypoints for special places where I want to return. I then upload the route to my computer, and the map is ready to go for my next trip."

While you might not be inclined to invest in a GPS if you're traveling a well-worn path, they can be indispensable for hikers, climbers, boaters, and back-road bicycle and motorcycle riders. They're also handy for drivers who are directionally challenged.

Laura uses hers for off-road motorcycle trips. "They're not good for planning because the screen's not big enough, but I use it like a backseat driver, someone who has knowledge of the local area. If I find myself going the wrong way, I can always find my way back through the waypoints."

If you choose a GPS that has a built-in personal digital assistant (PDA), it can help you track both your schedule and path. They also come with a built-in language translator. Some of the best-rated handheld versions come from Garmin (www.garmin.com). Prices can range from $100 to $1,000.

An added bonus of using a GPS is that you can get involved with geocaching! This is an outdoor treasure-hunting activity in which players find and hide "treasures" around the world using their GPS units. Through the Geocaching.com website (www.geocaching.com), you have access to caches worldwide. You find the stash of goods (typically inexpensive trinkets in a waterproof bottle) by using coordinates you acquire from the website and then key into your GPS; then you take something and leave something behind. Don't forget to make a note in the logbook!

What's Up in Downloads

Enjoy the latest in audio, text and video as they are delivered directly to your computer.

Audio Tours

Several companies are creating audio tours for destinations across the globe. You can listen to them before your trip to give you a sense of place prior to your departure, or you can use them to guide you through a city (on foot) once you arrive. Audio tours can be downloaded onto your iPod, laptop or other listening device.

iJourneys (www.ijourneys.com) offers numerous audio walking tours, including Ancient Rome and Pompeii. Owner Elyse Weiner says, "iJourneys are conducive for a woman traveling solo because she can walk through a city with her headset on, rather than with her head in a 600-page guide, screaming I'm a tourist!"

Soundwalk (www.soundwalk.com) provides cheery, techno-beat-backed audio tours that are actually quite fun to listen to. While the majority of their tours (including the Hip Hop Walk and the Hasidic Walk in Brooklyn) are located in New York City, Soundwalk also offers Train Away running tours, which guide you through cities such as Berlin and Paris as you jog.

✿ Podcasts

Podcasts are downloadable audio segments that are often free. Audio travel programs by publishers such as Lonely Planet and Rick Steves' Europe Through the Back Door (www.ricksteves. com) provide information on travel to specific destinations, including interviews with tour guides and travel diaries by professional reporters—or just travelers like you and me. Programs may be as short as 10 minutes or as long as an hour. Since podcasts are portable, you can listen to them while you're at the gym dreaming about your trip or while you're taking an overnight bus journey from Bangkok to Chang Mai.

You can also listen to interesting articles that include tips and reviews at Indie Travel Podcast (www.indietravelpodcast. com) or tune in to interviews at Amateur Traveler (www. amateurtraveler.com).

Hot Tip! With a small digital recorder or a simple accessory for your MP3 player, you can record sounds and create your own podcasts when you return home.

❧ RSS (Really Simple Syndication)

RSS feeds allow you to be instantly updated via an alert when one of your favorite websites or blogs adds a new post or announcement. I subscribe to travel alerts so that I know as soon as a special airfare has been announced or a newsworthy item is posted.

An RSS feed is a service you subscribe to from a specific website or even a particular subject on that site. These feeds use aggregator software supplied by Yahoo!, AOL, Google, Bloglines, or other providers.

Each time an update is added to the website or subject for which you have subscribed, it is added to your aggregator list, which is usually found on your RSS home page. Only the most recent feeds remain on your list, however, so for sites that update often, you'll need to check your feeds regularly (more than once a day).

Here's an example: SideStep offers RSS feeds so that you can be informed when there's a new deal listed for one of their travel options: hotel, cruises, timeshares, airfare, etc. By keeping an eye on your feed, you'll be informed as soon as these deals are announced.

As you're researching online, look for the RSS feed icon, and have your favorite subjects sent to you automatically.

❧ ebooks

Amazon and Sony (www.sonystyle.com) both manufacture ebook (electronic book) readers, devices onto which you can download full-length books and read them on-screen. Slightly smaller, but much thinner, than a paperback book, Amazon's Kindle can hold up to 200 books, and Sony's Reader Digital Book holds up to 160 books.

The units are pricey, at $350 for the Kindle and $300 for the Reader Digital Book. The downloadable books have to be purchased separately but are cheaper than the paper version. The Kindle comes with a power adapter, as well as a USB cable. Unless you're traveling with your laptop and can use the USB cable as a power source, you'll need to purchase the power adapter for the Reader Digital Book as it's sold separately.

✥ Videos

TotalVid (www.totalvid.com) has hundreds of travel-related videos available for download to your laptop or other device capable of using the Windows Media player. It works similarly to a rental in that you have a limited number of days to view the video, but the cost is a fraction of purchasing the DVD—and the sheer quantity of videos available on TotalVid is far greater than what your local video store can carry. Pssst . . . try Netflix (www.netflix.com) for a wide range of travel videos for rent delivered right to your door.

12.

LEGAL TENDER

BUDGETING. *Record keeping. Currency conversion. Tipping. Cash versus credit card. It can all seem mind boggling. With a little extra attention to your wallet, however, you can save some money and feel more confident in your travels.*

🌀 Saving for Your Journey

How much money you must dedicate for your trip is going to be tied to the length of your trip, how you'll spend your time, and the level of luxury or sacrifice with which you're comfortable. Before you budget for your journey, however, you must save for your journey. I've been asked many times over the last 20 years how I can afford to travel so much. It isn't because my Great Aunt left me a stash of dough in her will or because I invented the next great gizmo that every retail outlet is carrying. It's because travel is my priority.

When I first got the travel bug, I remember watching my co-workers go out to lunch every day, spending their hard-earned cash on food and drinks. Me? I brought my lunch and saved about $25 a week as a result (and was healthier for it, too). It may not sound like much, but when you're backpacking and a hostel in Bangkok costs about $2 a night and a meal from a street vendor approximately $1, that $25 adds about a week onto an adventure.

When travel becomes your priority, nothing else matters. That impulse buy at the jewelry store, the bottle of perfume you thought you couldn't live without, or the special dinner you want to splurge on can all be postponed and the cash tucked away in a special travel fund. Ask for cash on your next birthday to help finance your dream and, before you know it, you'll have squirreled away a few dollars here and there that add up rather quickly.

Hot Tip! Use a credit card that allows you to accumulate frequent flier miles for as many purchases as possible (including everyday expenditures, such as bill paying and groceries). However, always pay off your credit card debt monthly, and don't overspend with the excuse that it's OK because you're gaining mileage for buying that new dress.

✤ Calculating Your Budget

You can calculate your budget in one of two ways: Determine how much money you'll need for the adventure you've chosen, or figure out how much you'll have to spend, and base your trip on the amount of cash on hand. Read guidebooks to calculate the cost of meals (add a bit extra for inflation) and factor in transportation (buses, taxis, trains, etc.), as this can be one of the costliest portions of your travels.

Give yourself a daily food, entertainment, and transportation budget. When you find yourself with a little extra cash because you bargained down your hotel stay or ate at a farmers' market rather than a restaurant, treat yourself to a souvenir or a tour.

Most importantly, discipline yourself. Overspending and maxing out your credit card while on a trip will cause you major stress and post-trip depression when you return home. If you can't pass up a once-in-a-lifetime opportunity, then make a deal with yourself and compromise in order to take advantage of what's important. In other words, hop at the chance to take an unplanned tour to observe the orangutans of Sumatra, but cut back on an expensive meal or two to make up for the added tour expense.

The more you plan in advance, the less stress you'll encounter as you save (and spend) for your travels.

✤ Record-keeping on the Road

Keeping track of what you're spending while traveling will help curb your spending sprees. You'll quickly catch on to the fact that your daily mid-afternoon trip to the gelato shop could have paid for a really nice meal in an upscale restaurant.

I carry a very small spiral-bound notebook to track my purchases for anything for which I don't have a receipt. I then

12. LEGAL TENDER

155

enter all of my expenses into the back of my journal at the end of the day. Tracking and evaluating where you're spending your money will help you stretch what you do have throughout the trip.

If you're a business traveler, you will need to get a receipt for every purchase. Use your credit or debit card when possible, so that you have an accounting of expenditures. This way, if you lose a receipt or don't receive one, you'll have a record of the purchase. Organize receipts by date so that when you return home you can file an expense report with your company quickly or add them to your own receipts if you have your own business.

Hot Tip! Designate a special place in your daypack, luggage or briefcase to "file" your receipts. This will help make record-keeping much easier both on the road and when you return home.

⚘ Money Changing

Consider having some of your cash converted to the local currency prior to your trip. American Express (www.americanexpress.com) allows you to order currency online for more than 50 destinations and then receive your cash via UPS delivery. They accept Visa, MasterCard and . . . you guessed it, American Express. However, the exchange rate you receive once you arrive at your destination will likely be better (unless the local currency is going through wild fluctuations) than if you change prior to leaving, so only get enough to get you to your hotel (taxi, tips, bellhop, etc.), and perhaps to pay for a bite to eat.

To get the best exchange rate while traveling, withdraw money directly from a bank with a debit card. If an ATM machine is unavailable, you can exchange cash or travelers checks at a bank (preferred) or an exchange bureau (they'll tack on extra fees). As a final option, you may be able to pay in U.S. dollars (USD), but often the store, restaurant, or hotel is sure to give you the absolute worst rate.

You may, on occasion, be asked to change your money on the streets as part of the black market. Typically, a shady character lurking outside a bank will offer to change your dollars into the local currency, offering you a better exchange rate than the bank. Seem too good to be true? It is! Though Mildred is a seasoned traveler, she couldn't resist the temptation to change USD $10 with a street changer in South America. "These conniving people were looking for stupid tourists, and it ended up the currency they gave us was phony. It's a smart thing to stay clear of anyone who is trying to change money in the streets. Luckily, I only lost a little."

Prior to leaving the country you're visiting, get the local currency exchanged back into U.S. dollars at a bank or exchange bureau. Save some cash for a departure tax, last-minute souvenirs, or a snack at the airport. (Check your guidebook to determine whether a departure tax is required, and the amount, or ask upon your arrival at the airport.) Some countries, such as Laos, won't allow you to leave with their currency; even if you could, the exchange rate at home would definitely not be in your favor.

Cash

While cash is king, it's not safe to carry large amounts of it when you're traveling. It's easy to lose, it's tempting for thieves, and there's no way to retrieve it, as there is with credit and debit cards or travelers checks, if something does happen to it.

Of course, you'll want to carry enough to get you through at least a few days of travel, or until you can get to another location to make an exchange or withdrawal. While ATMs generally have 24-hour access, banks may have very different schedules than what you are used to. For example, expect banks in Europe to close in the early afternoon, and be prepared for long lunch breaks (siestas) in countries in Central and South America.

In some cases, having cash can be a boon. In Costa Rica for instance, hotels, gift shops and restaurants will reduce your bill by a percentage if you pay in U.S. dollars. And "cash" includes travelers checks.

Many, but not all, shops abroad will accept U.S. currency. Generally, those who work in the hospitality industry and are used to interactions with travelers, will happily accept U.S. dollars, especially if you've just arrived at the airport. I carry enough cash in U.S. dollars to pay for a taxi or bus to my hotel once I've landed, as well as enough singles to tip everyone from the bellhop to the street vendor who may provide me with a particularly memorable meal. Depending on the strength of the U.S. dollar, even non-U.S. citizens should consider carrying the greenback. Hotels and restaurants in some countries even charge in U.S. dollars, rather than the local currency, making payment easy, with no currency conversion necessary.

Bills need to be in good, crisp shape. In some countries, store owners will hand you back a bill that is torn or well worn. Before any trip, I spend 10 minutes at my bank going through singles to find the best ones for tips and small purchases.

Credit Cards

While credit cards are far more convenient than cash, don't be surprised if there are additional fees tacked on by your bank.

Charges vary from bank to bank, but factor in 3 percent for every purchase, and be happy if it's anything less. Capital One, a rare exception, does not tack on this surcharge.

Before you get all crazy with your money and start using your credit card for cash advances, be aware that these withdrawals often include a transaction fee, as well as interest rates as high as 25 percent.

Carry the non-toll-free phone number for your credit-card company and bank in case you need to contact them because toll-free numbers don't work outside of North America. Fortunately, these companies will accept collect calls.

Hot Tip! If purchasing souvenirs from a factory or shop that ships them home for you, it's a good idea to purchase items by credit card, in case they get lost or damaged.

Debit Cards/Cash Machines

When you need local currency, you will get the best exchange rate by making a withdrawal from a bank's ATM. These are prolific in cities and larger towns, but don't expect to find them in remote areas, especially in developing countries. Have cash as a backup.

When she knew she'd be traveling to far-flung areas of India, Amy was prepared for worse-case scenarios. "I would take $800 out of an ATM, and that would cover me if I had to stay at the most expensive hotels every night for three weeks, until I got to the next ATM."

Keep in mind that your bank may charge a fee (as much as $5) for using your debit card on machines not affiliated with them.

❧ Travelers Checks

While not as widely used as they once were, due to the popularity of debit and credit cards, travelers checks can come in handy in some countries. And, despite what some commercials might have you think, Visa is not accepted everywhere.

American Express offers travelers checks in local currency, which you can get prior to your departure. There may be a fee for this transaction, and the exchange rate will be based on the day you actually purchase the checks. These are helpful if you're going to one region where only one currency is used (i.e. one country or to the European Union).

Leave copies of the numbers for your travelers checks both at home and in your luggage. If you get separated from both your money and your luggage, you'll still have access to this info.

Convert your travelers checks at a bank, rather than at a change bureau. A *bureau de change* or *casa de cambio*, which are popular terms for these exchange locations, may not only charge you a fee, but you'll probably get a less favorable rate than from a bank.

In developing countries, spotty or nonexistent electricity make it impossible to rely on ATMs or credit-card processing machines in shops and restaurants. Beyond these obvious infrastructure issues, power outages can happen anywhere, making travelers checks a good backup.

❧ Currency Converters

Calculate exchange rates prior to your departure at XE.com (www.xe.com). This tool is invaluable when booking online in the local currency for your hotel, package tour, or local events.

Handheld currency converters are also available for about USD $15, and they often include a calculator and alarm clock. Magellan's Travel Supplies carries a variety of these.

❀ Bargaining

Bargaining can be an exhilarating experience, whether you are at the traditional Indian market in Chichicastenango, Guatemala, or a flea market in a parking lot in Birmingham, Alabama. It's a perfect opportunity to interact with the locals.

I window shop before I begin any bargaining adventure. I search fixed-price stores to get an idea of how much an item costs, and I get used to the currency so that I can do quick calculations.

Broadly speaking, sellers will ask double the amount they are actually willing to accept for their item. Depending on your skill at bargaining and desire for the article, you might be able to bargain down to half price. If a seller asks a very high price for something, I walk away, knowing that he isn't serious about selling that day.

Vendors in developing countries will tell you, "Westerners are short on time and long on money, while we're short on money and long on time." In other words, they have all the time in the world to make their sale, while you will undoubtedly give up far too quickly in order to save yourself time.

While it can seem petty to bargain over a few cents or a few dollars for a souvenir, bargaining is more than just saving money. It's a chance to connect with the locals, and the seller is not going to sell you something at a loss. Allow the back and forth to happen, write down your offer on a piece of paper (or in the dirt if need be), and let the seller make a counter offer. Stay patient, feign disinterest, but continue to haggle. If you're not serious about purchasing something, don't waste a

Bargaining Mishap

In Cambodia, while bargaining with a taxi driver for the cost of a half-day trip along a deserted road to Angkor Wat, I was reduced to writing in the dirt to ensure that we were in the same ballpark in terms of cost. We were both speaking English, but what I heard was 17,000 riels, and what he was actually saying was 70,000!–BW

vendor's time by giving him or her false hope of a sale. Once you begin bargaining, see the purchase through if a fair price is offered.

And, while you participate in bargaining, remember that your purchase just might determine how much the vendor's family eats that evening. Be willing to pay what the item is worth to you.

If you discover that you've made too many purchases on your trip (gifts for yourself, perhaps), consider shipping them home. On my first trip to Thailand, I apparently forgot a tiny detail: the fact that I was at the beginning of a year-long trip. I was so enamored by the indigenous crafts and beautiful tapestries that I overbought and had to ship a box of items to my parents' home. I made a list of everything included in the box, and once I returned home, it was like Christmas to see all the items I had purchased nearly a year earlier.

Haggling isn't limited to the sale of goods. Ask for a lower room rate or a discount on your tour. Wait for an opportune moment to ask for a better deal when no other customers are around. A hotel clerk will more likely work with you on a price if they don't feel that others are listening.

If the price is fixed on a hotel room, ask for the best-available room in that price range or a complementary upgrade. By simply asking, perhaps you'll get a larger room or one with a view of the beach.

❧ Tipping

Tipping varies tremendously around the world. North Americans are used to 15 to 20 percent as a standard tip, while an Italian taxi driver will be happy with 5 to 10 percent, and a German waiter with 10 percent. In many countries, the tip is included in the bill. Your guidebook will provide info on local tipping customs. Unless you don't mind parting with your cash, check the bill, or simply ask if the tip is included.

❧ Tax Refunds

Many countries allow nonresident tourists to apply for a refund on value-added tax (VAT) for purchases they take home. This tax can be as much as 25 percent. For up-to-date information and a list of participating countries, Global Refund (www. globalrefund.com) is a good resource. Requirements differ slightly with every country. For example, you must purchase at least USD $25 worth of goods in Sweden to qualify. In Switzerland it's $340—and some countries, such as Canada, will allow a refund on your hotel stay, while other countries allow it only for merchandise.

To apply for your refund, you must receive the VAT paperwork from the store or hotel where you make your purchase. Not all shops will have the proper paperwork, in which case you are out of luck. Look for the tax-free shopping logo in the window, as they will be VAT-paperwork-friendly.

12. LEGAL TENDER

When departing from the airport, show the VAT paperwork, your receipt, and the goods (don't put them in your checked luggage) to customs officials, and they will validate your form with a stamp. Often, there will be a tax-free shopping desk at the airport where you can get an immediate cash refund. Otherwise, you can submit the form by mail or through an on-line service, such as Global Refund or Tax Back International (www.taxbackinternational. com), which will submit the paperwork on your behalf for a fee.

If you purchase goods at a tax-free shop (we've all seen duty-free stores in the international terminals at airports), you can submit your receipt to a designated tax-free shopping desk on-site or get a refund by mail.

If you've made a lot of purchases and were diligent about keeping receipts, you could easily get a refund totaling hundreds of dollars. Not a bad way to help offset some of the cost of your trip.

❧ Money-saving Tips

- Share rides to and from the airport with other travelers.

- When you meet a traveler you like, ask to share a room or a ride to your next destination.

- Stay in hotels where breakfast is included.

- Always ask for a better price, no matter what you are purchasing.

- Look over your receipts at restaurants, hotels, grocery stores, and shops to make sure you haven't been overcharged.

13.

SAFETY FIRST

TRAVELING *solo does not mean that your travels will be less safe than if you were traveling with others. It does mean, however, that you must stay alert, implement extra safety measures, and make decisions based on the fact that you are on your own.*

🖋 Safety and Your Destination

Friends and family are eager to inform us about the rare negative instances (assaults, rapes, etc.) that make the news. However, bad things happen to good people *everywhere*, whether they are traveling or in their own hometown. It's uncommon for a woman traveler to encounter an outright dangerous situation, particularly when being cautious.

While travel is very safe statistically, there are issues that specifically affect solo women travelers. Getting groped on public transportation or being exposed to bravado behavior by a group of local men are among the hassles you may encounter. Some might suspect that you are looking for a romantic liaison. And, depending on where you travel, you may find a general lack of understanding and subsequent disrespect for a gal traveling on her own.

🖋 Travel Warnings

Travel warnings are issued by the U.S. Department of State for countries they recommend Americans avoid. This is an excellent starting point if you have concerns regarding a specific destination.

Take the information with a grain of salt, however, as some countries may be listed as "unsafe" when, in reality, there may be just isolated pockets of areas that should be avoided. Consider the fact that after the 2002 bombing in Kuta, Bali, the country of Indonesia was placed on this list. In direct contrast, the U.S. government actually encouraged travel to New York and Washington, D.C. after the September 11 attacks. Where's the fairness in that?

Read current news accounts, and research newspapers and the Internet for the most up-to-date information.

✿ Crime Rates

Safety levels vary tremendously from country to country, and even within one. While some destinations have a reputation for being less safe than others, it's usually a specific area of a city that deserves the reputation (such as the Medina of Marrakesh at night) or during a certain time of year (Rio de Janeiro during Carnival).

Information for domestic and international crime rates is spotty at best, and may not reflect the exact area to which you will be traveling. For example, crime rates for New York may encompass the entire city, while you may only want to visit Greenwich Village, which is considered relatively safe.

I'm definitely not comfortable being stared at or prompted to respond to advances from strange men, but I won't let that deter me from traveling where I choose. This is a personal choice. You will need to make destination decisions based on your comfort level for potential inappropriate attention from locals, as well as the overall safety factor of an area.

Several resources can help you make decisions about whether a region is acceptable for you and help you steer clear of those with a bad reputation. Read guidebooks for an overview of the general hassle factor for women; and check out online forums (see Chapter 4, Mapping Out the Details) for not only up-to-the-minute information on safety concerns for your destination, but also details about how you can protect yourself against specific scams. Sometimes, just being aware of what latest tricks a con artist or thief is employing is enough to stay out of harm's way since you'll know what to watch for.

Be very private in terms of the information that you give out. An innocent conversation with another female traveler in a public place could be overheard by someone with less-than honorable intentions, allowing them to find out where you're staying and for how long.

While it is important to have your guard up, it will be equally important to be open to the experiences that travel has to offer, as well as to trust locals and other travelers you encounter.

❧ Clothing Choices

Understanding the local culture is the first step in thwarting unwanted stares, cat calls, advances, sexual harassment, or potential assaults. In no way am I suggesting that the victim is at fault. However, when traveling in conservative countries such as India or the Middle East, showing your elbows or wearing shorts could be considered promiscuous, leading to unwanted attention.

For solo women travelers, there is probably no better piece of advice I can give than to dress conservatively. Know what is considered appropriate attire for your destination, and follow the advice of those who've gone before you. In countries where machismo prevails, you will still feel the burning eyes of men watching you with intrigue (and/or perhaps disdain). By not dressing provocatively (by their standards) you'll feel more comfortable and will be safer.

Hot Tip! To stave off unwanted advances from men, wear a wedding ring (fake, if need be), carry a photo of your "husband", and have a good story ready as to why he isn't with you at that moment.

❧ Demeanor Counts

Traveling with confidence is a major component in how safe your travels will be. It could mean the difference between someone snagging your luggage at a railway station or a thief passing you over because you're alert, holding onto your bags, and holding yourself upright. If you don't feel confident, consider taking a self-defense class to build your confidence and to help you learn to be vigilantly aware of your surroundings and personal items.

While you certainly won't want to be flirtatious, flashing a smile and standing up straight will help give you an air of assurance. Smiling, in general, will get you a long way, and will make your travels that much more pleasant, as people will respond positively to you.

During her six months of studying the tea industry in India, Amy knew how to best present herself. "Rather than just wandering around, I came off as a professional, dedicated to what I was working on. I always trusted my gut."

❧ A Word About us Women

Women have the good fortune to be endowed with a sixth sense, a gut instinct for both the good and the bad. Tuning into and trusting this intuition is critical to having a safe journey. It may be the reason you readily accept a dinner invitation with a gentleman you meet on a train, yet turn down an invite from a fellow traveler to accompany him on a two-day hike through the Brazilian rainforest.

I've spoken with countless women who, even after months of traveling on their own, admitted to doing irresponsible things during their adventures by letting their guard down. They divulged that they felt like something was wrong from the beginning, whether it was getting into a taxi with a driver who couldn't be trusted, or accepting a "private tour" to the center of a pyramid in Egypt by a less-than-savory character. One woman accepted a ride from the airport, only to be taken to the driver's apartment. She escaped, even though she had been held at knifepoint.

These situations can be avoided if you remain aware and give yourself permission to say "no" at the slightest feeling that something might be amiss. Often, as women, we are afraid of offending others. By overcoming this fear, you can speak firmly to the person(s) bothering you and remove yourself immediately from the situation.

If you sense that something's wrong, it probably is. It's important to trust your instincts, even if you have to turn down what appears to be a once-in-a-lifetime opportunity. Over time, whether on the road or at home, you'll know when you're being paranoid and when your gut is right. Learn to trust yourself, and soon the feeling will come naturally.

And, by the way, once-in-a-lifetime opportunities happen every day when you're traveling!

Hotel Safety

While you may feel safest in your hotel, don't allow a false sense of security to catch you with your guard down. Staying alert and honoring your gut feelings about situations could well prevent problems.

When booking your hotel, ask the hotel staff about how safe the area is; there's a good chance they'll be honest with you if you explain that you're on your own.

At check in, if the hotel clerk says your room number out loud and there are others in the lobby, ask for another room and request that he or she write down the number. This is the easiest place for others to notice that you are traveling on your own, and you won't want them to know where to find you.

Rooms closer to the elevator or stairs, while potentially noisier, will be safer than rooms at the far end of a floor or down a side wing. The more people and traffic around, the better chance someone will hear you if you need help.

If you feel uncomfortable in the room that's been assigned to you, don't hesitate to request a different one. Perhaps there's someone creepy next door, maybe the lock doesn't work properly, or perhaps it wasn't cleaned well. You're paying for it; ensure that you're comfortable.

Once in the room, keep the door locked and only open it if you've ordered room service or requested an item such as an iron or new remote—and then only after you've checked through the peep hole to confirm that it's actually hotel staff. If someone you're not expecting knocks, call down to the front desk to confirm that the person is with the hotel.

If there are no locks (such as a deadbolt) in addition to the doorknob lock, place a piece of furniture against the door. Even if it isn't heavy enough to prevent someone from entering, you'll be alerted if someone tries to get in. While on a trip through Central America, I kept a chair in front of the door and a high-decibel alarm next to the bed. These alarms come on a small keychain, and are activated when you pull a pin (hand grenade-style) from the unit. If someone were to enter the room, I would have been awakened by the chair and could have sounded the alarm to bring attention to the situation.

In less-modern hotels, the key will be on a large keychain to prevent you from losing it. The keychain, however, may include the name of your hotel and room number. If you lose it, someone could easily find and enter your room. Remove the key from the chain to avoid this issue, and then keep the key in a safe place.

Leave the "Do Not Disturb" sign on your door even when you're not in the room, and keep the TV or radio on while you're out to give the appearance of someone being inside. This will dissuade thieves, who will presume the room is occupied. Also, do not leave out the "Please Clean" sign, as this will signal that the room is vacant.

Hot Tip! Carry a rubber door stop. If the door doesn't have a chain lock, slip the stopper underneath it to prevent intruders from entering with a key.

While incidents are less common than they were just 10 years ago, corrupt police have been known to plant illicit drugs in tourists' rooms or merely threaten to do so, in order to receive a bribe. Destinations with the most common reports of this abuse are India, Southeast Asia, and Russia.

If you hear or read that this may be an issue where you're traveling, you can take measures to deter it. When you leave your room, place a piece of tape over your hotel door and the frame of the door, or slip a piece of paper between the door and frame. When you get back to your room, you'll be able to tell if someone has been inside by checking whether the tape or paper have been moved.

If you believe that someone has entered your room while you were out, call the hotel manager immediately for help.

✻ Transportation

Riding public transportation can be tiring. Your senses will be overstimulated by the people, sights, sounds, and smells, and you may find yourself tempted to let down your guard. If there

ꜰꜰꜰ Mary's Story ꜰꜰꜰ

I had a run-in once at a hotel in Assisi, which you would think would be safe due to all the pilgrims there. I was checked in to the hotel in the morning by a grandfather and his two grand-daughters. When I left for the day to sightsee, I left the key at the desk because it was on one of those big key chains so you won't leave with the key.

In the evening when I returned, a young man in his 20s who spoke English was behind the desk, and had glasses of wine wait-ing for himself and me. I asked for my room key and he didn't want to return it to me. Instead, he suggested that we go to my room. I just kept talking to him, drank my wine, and then tricked him by asking him for more wine. When he went to get more in the kitchen, I grabbed the key and ran upstairs.

Once in the room, I put the key through the keyhole on my side and then put a chair up against it so he couldn't get a key in or push my key out, as there was no deadbolt.

I was panicked, because he was talking to me from the hallway. I pretended to make a phone call, even though I didn't have any-one to call. I made up a conversation so he would think I knew someone local, and if something happened to me, the other per-son would know. I didn't want him to think I was scared, and in-stead told him, through the door, that I would see him tomorrow. I then just made light conversation on the phone about what I did all day.

By appearing calm and not letting him know I was afraid, I felt in power of the situation. Eventually, he gave up and went back downstairs.

The next day, I packed up everything and left.

was ever a time to stay alert, it's when you're in a crowd and easily distracted.

While riding on a heavily packed Metro subway in Mexico City, I found myself being groped and rubbed up against by the men by whom I was surrounded. I had learned a few words of Spanish for this first trip to Mexico. In a voice just loud enough for these men and some other passengers nearby to hear me, I said "*Basta, pendejo.*" (Enough, stupid person.) Since it's not common for a woman to speak up in such a situation, I was immediately rewarded with a two-inch buffer between myself and everyone around me.

Determine an "exit strategy" before you find yourself stuck in the middle of a crowded bus or train. Whether it's saying something in the local language to discourage further groping or hopping off at the nearest stop, don't hesitate to stand up for yourself.

It might take a bit of reconditioning, as we are taught to be "nice," but talking back, preferably loud enough so that others can hear, is often enough to intimidate someone from bothering you further.

While you're on public transportation, lock your luggage to a fixed point (such as a seat) with a bicycle cable and lock. These pliable locks will keep your things safe while you nap on long rides. Pacsafe sells a luggage protector made of wire mesh that slips over your bag to prevent theft of your bags' contents. It also includes a lock.

If you plan to snooze, secure your bags' zippers together with small locks or even a key ring slipped through both zippers. This will be a good first line of defense in thwarting a casual thief looking for an easy steal.

Hot Tip! If traveling by car, lock your luggage in the trunk with a cable lock to ensure your bags won't get ripped off.

❀ Walking

If the area is safe and you plan to go out for the evening on foot, attempt to connect with other travelers, as there will be safety in numbers. Always have enough cash on hand so you can catch a cab. If they are not readily available from the street, ask for help in calling a taxi from a restaurant or shop.

When walking down a street, look for crowds you can attach yourself to by walking "with" them, continuously scanning the sidewalks and road. Stay alert to anyone who might be following you. Cross the street if an unsavory character appears to be heading your way.

Hot Tip! Once you arrive at your destination, buy mace or pepper spray for protection.

If you feel threatened, slide your keys between your knuckles as a weapon, and be prepared to defend yourself. As women, we are not wired to be as aggressive as men, and therefore we need to prepare ourselves emotionally as well as physically to hurt another person for our own safety.

Cheri, a program and sales director, found herself in a precarious position while she was walking down an alley in Nice, France. A drunk man was approaching from the other direction and speaking to her in French, which she couldn't understand. While he seemed threatening, Cheri wasn't intimidated. "I held up my fists and yelled for him to back off, and that was enough to scare him away." How does she stay safe? "I walk with confidence." At first glance, you wouldn't think that this woman with an Ivory-girl look could deter a threatening drunk, but the way she holds herself is all confidence.

Sue travels often to pursue her love of music, and has found herself in some undesirable neighborhoods while searching for music venues. Her advice is: "Don't look startled. If you run into someone who is somewhat predatory, the minute you look panicky, you've lost it. They recognize you as a potential victim, and you're much more likely to be mugged. Don't give off the vibe, don't engage in conversation, and just keep walking." Avoiding higher risk areas to begin with will help you steer clear of problems. If it's someplace you must go, take a taxi and travel with others.

The power of copping an attitude and expressing confidence cannot be underestimated. Take a class in self-defense and don't be intimidated to protect yourself. Sometimes all it takes is showing a small amount of strength to discourage a would-be thief or attacker.

Theft

Luggage and Bags—Losing your luggage can be disastrous at best, and trip ending, at worst. You will have taken great care at packing your precious items, likely including a few things that you covet (perhaps a new digital camera or iPod). To have them stolen because you left them unattended for a brief moment or in the care of a porter you thought you could trust would be heart-wrenching. The worst thing I've ever had stolen was a $10 travel alarm that I left out in the open. It's not that I've just been lucky; I'm vigilant about knowing where my bags are at all times, and keeping them locked up.

In your hotel, keep your valuables secured in your bags and your bags locked to something stationary in the room, such as the bed. It may seem overly cautious, but you can bet that anyone who has ever lost a video camera, jewelry, or passport would beg to differ. Most hotel staff members are quite trustworthy, but there may be bad apples who have a key to your room, so it's best to be safe.

If you plan to sleep in a public area, such as on a train, make doubly sure that nothing can be easily opened or taken. Wrap the straps of your daypack around your wrists to prevent a quick snatching.

While living in London on a work assignment, Maricris traveled throughout Europe on her own each month for pleasure. She wasn't comfortable carrying a daypack. "When I had a daypack, I felt more vulnerable than having a bag that went across my body and sat under my arm." Using a messenger-bag type of carry-all can dissuade thieves, as they can't lift anything out of the bag or snatch it completely.

At restaurants and cafés, particularly if they are outdoors, never place your bag on the floor where you could easily forget it. Instead, keep your bag strapped to you by positioning the strap over your head and one arm. Alternatively, you could wrap the strap around your leg or the leg of your chair. When seated, keep your wallet, change purse, sunglasses, or any other small items in your bag or pockets. They are too easily forgotten or stolen when sitting on the table. While this may sound like common sense, I have heard many stories of items being stolen off of tables because the person absent-mindedly left them out in the open.

Money—A money belt or neck pouch will keep your passport, credit cards, and cash safe and close to your body, so you will always know they are there. I keep items I don't need to access immediately in a money belt and larger items (such as

Motorcycle Man

When I was riding on the back of my friend, Kim's, motorbike in Saigon, a man on a large motorcycle flashed me. This happened not once, but three times, as he rode alongside us. No one else on the busy street seemed to notice, and Kim, who is Vietnamese, had her eyes fixed on the road while I frantically tried to explain to her what was happening.

Not having learned the word for "penis" in Vietnamese, I was unable to explain to Kim that we were being followed by an exhibitionist, and my frantic gesturing was lost on her. In hopes that he would leave us alone, I started yelling to draw attention to him, and he finally rode away. In looking back, I suppose a simple laughing gesture on my part may have shooed him away even faster.–BW

a camera) and cash I plan to spend that day in a daypack or messenger-type bag. While money belts aren't necessarily inconspicuous, they do not tempt thieves like a wallet, purse, or small bag might.

Paperwork

Keep copies of all important documents in your luggage, as well as copies at home and even copies in your email account. This includes passports, visas, plane tickets (or e-tickets), hotel reservations, bus or train tickets, travelers checks, contact numbers, and phone numbers for your bank or credit-card companies. If your luggage gets stolen with these documents, you'll have a backup set at home and they'll be accessible online if you've scanned them and emailed them to yourself. Refer to Chapter 8, Red Tape and Formalities, for more details.

✣ Police and Officials

If you encounter a problem in which the police need to be involved, you may not be able to properly convey the issue at hand, due to a language barrier. If you can't explain the problem, the police may be dismissive of your case. It may be worth the time and money to find an interpreter through your embassy. Your credit-card company, for instance, will require a police report before reimbursing you for a purchase guaranteed under their loss-protection policy.

If you are in a region where the authorities have a reputation for being less than honorable, take special care to avoid them. On rare occasions, the police, military, and other officials (or those purporting to represent them) may be more corrupt

Dealing with Authority

While I was traveling solo through Central America on my motorcycle, I had to stop often for the police at state borders in Mexico, at country borders, and on the highway when the police were just curious who was riding a BMW F650 through their country. (Panamanian police were particularly charming. Not only did they speak perfect English, but they only pulled me over to look at my bike.)

In broken Spanish, I explained that my husband and I were studying Spanish in . . . (I named the next big city) and that we loved this country (whichever one I was in) very much. While I (almost) never felt threatened by these policemen, providing a story that they could relate to made my odd appearance seem almost normal, and they allowed me to continue on without hassle. It didn't hurt that I offered compliments and was very friendly.–BW than the citizens of a country. Guidebooks and online forums will provide information about such locations.

It's common to find police checkpoints in Brazil and Mexico, and, depending on the current political situation, Nepal, India, and Thailand also often have checkpoints in some regions. When traveling on public transportation wherein checkpoints are common, lie low and don't draw attention to yourself.

If you're driving your own vehicle, it may not be safe to pull over for what appears to be an unmarked police car. In North America, dial 911 or stop in an area with lots of people if in doubt about who is actually pulling you over. When traveling abroad, only stop where there are many people around to ensure your safety. If you do find yourself in trouble with the police, demand to call your embassy immediately for advice.

And, if you are the victim of a crime, notify your nearest embassy or consulate, which will be listed in your guidebook. Consular agents can help with replacing your passport, contacting your family, getting you medical care, and obtaining an attorney for you.

14.

GETTING ACQUAINTED

ONE *of the most interesting and exciting parts of travel is encountering new people from around the world. Whether you meet other travelers also visiting your destination or you befriend locals once you arrive, these new friends are sure to make your travels memorable. While it doesn't take a lot of energy to meet others, sometimes it does take a conscious effort. Here are some things you can do to ease yourself into the process.*

ꕤ Meeting Locals

Everyone you come into contact with on the road is a potential new friend. As you travel solo, hotel staff will see that you are on your own and be friendlier, the barista or wait staff from the coffee shop will welcome the chance to chat with a new-comer, and a compliment to the chef may get you invited into the kitchen. If you're staying in one spot for a few days and you're seen making nice with the locals, this could very well save you from being hassled by any neighborhood thugs.

Betty Ann, who traveled to 70 countries in her nine years as a tour guide, learned quickly how to connect with people. "Talk to your cab driver or the guest-services person at the hotel to learn about their favorite restaurant, or ask your guide where he or she would go. If you ask, "Where's your favorite spot?' many people will open up because you want to get to know about their life rather than just going where the guidebooks suggest."

Become a Regular—If you're staying in one location for more than a few days, you can often make local friends if you fre-quent the same place for coffee or meals. You'll have a better chance of being remembered if you are warm, friendly, and ask questions.

While teaching English in Saigon for two months, I stopped by a small café each day for a *mang cau* shake. Not only did I love the sweetness of this fresh fruit drink, but I made fast friends with the two gals who ran the shop (and I put on a few pounds, as well).

Ask Questions—If you're traveling to a non-English-speak-ing country, it's easier than you think to meet locals. With

Locals to the Rescue

I have had many challenging experiences in my travels when I have come out feeling stronger, and I have met some wonderful locals. One such time was during a motorcycle ride through New Mexico on my way to Central America. I thought the road was just in really bad shape (which it was), causing my bike to be slightly unbalanced. Unbeknownst to me, however, my tire had been punctured by a nail on this desolate, twisty road. With a mountain face on one side and a sheer drop into a creek bed on the other, I had no place to pull over to examine my bike and had to press on. Ten miles later, I happened upon a lone real estate office at a juncture in the road, and stopped for help.

The employees came to my rescue by calling in the closest (boat) mechanic, 30 miles away. On this late Saturday afternoon with most shops closed, the mechanic ordered a new tire tube from Albuquerque (an hour away), sent his brother to pick it up, and loaned me his personal car for the night so I could get back to the youth hostel. I returned the next day for my bike and to settle the bill, which totaled just $100.

I could have easily crashed on a flat tire, and my trip would have been over. Having this near-disastrous event just prior to crossing the Mexican border should have been enough to make me return home. But the generosity and caring that these strangers showed me was so encouraging that I was able to continue. I had the confidence of knowing that I could overcome any issues, and that there would always be people to help along this journey. What I've discovered over the years, but occasionally still have to remind myself, is that more often than not, fellow travelers and locals will come to the rescue in a traveler's time of need.—BW the exception of the most remote areas, someone will speak English. And if you can't find someone who can understand you, take the opportunity to crack open your phrasebook, and practice the local language. Start with your hotel clerk, waitress or taxi driver, all of whom may provide you with insight into their culture if you just start asking questions.

Volunteer—Volunteering (covered in Chapter 2, Travel Idea Generator), can be a splendid way to meet other people and occupy your time if you'll be spending more than a few days in one location. Offer to help out in a hospital, orphanage, or school once you arrive. If you have a special skill, such as in medicine, teaching or cooking, present your services to an appropriate facility. To save money and meet lots of people, you may even be able to "volunteer" at your hotel or guest house, or at the neighborhood café in exchange for room and board or free meals.

Other Travelers

The majority of travelers won't stray far off the beaten path, so it's fairly predictable where to find them: in hostels, Internet cafés, coffee or tea shops, and even hotel lobbies. Websites and guidebooks can also point you in the direction of the best places to meet up with other travelers. While online resources will be the most up-to-date, the Lonely Planet guides are by far the most comprehensive for this type of information.

Eat out where you know other travelers will be, and you'll quickly make friends. And taking a day trip with a tour company will place you among a group of travelers, many of whom will also be traveling solo.

Higher-end hotels generally have restaurants and bars where you can relax, read, and enjoy a drink or a bite to eat. While many people will be transient, not sitting for long periods of time, you'll probably meet a few travelers who are guests, and you might even stumble upon some employees who are travelers themselves, but working on a temporary basis. I've spent many an afternoon in hotel cafés around the world catching up on my writing and chatting with passersby.

If you're bashful about introducing yourself, be prepared with a conversation starter by introducing a timely topic or asking for ideas about what sights to see.

While in France by herself, Mary Jo discovered that tables were placed so close together that she could often overhear conversations. When she heard English being spoken, she found a way to politely insert herself into the conversation so others would know that she, too, spoke English. She soon found herself meeting new people.

Oftentimes, people will want to talk to you simply because you're on your own. Susan celebrated her divorce with a backroad U.S. trip, and met lots of people along the way. "I was the object of curiosity, and people would take me in because I was by myself. I would meet couples and families while hiking, and they would then invite me to their campsite for dinner."

Romantic Relationships

You might find the love of your life during your travels, or you may get involved with a short-term fling. Regardless of your intentions, being prepared both physically and emotionally will ease the cultural miscues and awkwardness that could overshadow an affair while you're traveling.

14. GETTING ACQUAINTED

185

✿✿✿ Sue's Story ✿✿✿

My first real travel experiences began when I was getting involved in music. I became fascinated with American roots music, particularly bluegrass, in other areas of the United States. I was doing research and started taking vacations to discover bluegrass for myself.

On one trip, I registered for the International Bluegrass Music Association Conference and had no idea what to expect. I flew into Louisville, Kentucky, and rented a car. Driving across the state to Owensboro, where the conference was, I went through small towns. There were churches on every corner of every town, and the food was not my usual fare: mostly fried catfish and corndogs . . . and grits for breakfast.

I had to get over the tendency to jump to conclusions about other people. People had missing teeth and they didn't dress like me. They sat on front porches on old rusty chairs, threadbare couches, and porch swings. This was their daily entertainment and a foundation of their community.

When I got to Owensboro, I made friends with a number of people from the bluegrass community who filled in the human elements of the sketches I'd seen on the road.

Jeannette Belliveau, author of *Romance on the Road: Traveling Women Who Love Foreign Men*, says, "Ideally, you should give some thought to how to politely put off annoying men and politely engage with intriguing guys—just as you would at home."

Unless you are already deeply acquainted with a culture, it will be difficult to comprehend the nuances of your romantic interest's verbal and nonverbal communication. If you become involved with someone from the country you're visiting, observe the behavior of the locals and act accordingly. Flagrant

I went to Louisville on vacation a couple of years later, and saw and learned a lot. I noticed the Bible Doll Museum in a small house along the road, and had to stop. I couldn't imagine what it was. It ended up being a heart-wrenching situation. A woman answered the door, and her husband was laid up on a cot on a respirator in the living room. She had made all these clothes for dolls and dressed them as characters from the Bible and placed them in scenes from Bible stories in a big room in her garage. This was her devotional to God for keeping her husband alive. She showed them to elementary-school students, and was thrilled when anyone came by to see her. It validated her work. I was honored to be there, and had to throw out all my pre-conceptions. I felt a little silly, and very moved.

When I travel, I tend to find someone with similar interests who is comfortable to be around. I just strike up conversations with people I meet along the way and then get introduced to other people. This leads to more and more introductions if you stay open to it. I like to think that I attract small adventures through meeting people and being passionate about things, and then following trails to more people and things to do.

14. GETTING ACQUAINTED

public displays of affection in a Muslim country won't get you far if you're trying to impress his family members. And an openly lesbian relationship may be okay in London, but not in Bogotá.

As a lesbian traveler, Andrea is more careful with regards to her sexual preference when she travels to an unfamiliar area. "I'm more cautious if I don't know the acceptance level. I respect the places I'm going to and act appropriately."

Falling in love is no excuse for having unprotected sex if you aren't sure your partner is disease-free. STDs and AIDS don't require a passport or visa to travel the world. Whether the relationship is long-term or a fling, use protection! Take condoms with you, as they may not be readily available in your travels, and if they are, they may not be up to Western standards. At one time, Saigon had dozens of outdoor street vendors selling condoms in the blazing-hot sun. I've always expected another baby-boom generation from Vietnam, as the quality of these condoms was surely dubious.

Be honest with the person about your feelings and your plans to stick around or continue traveling. Realize that he or she may not have the same economic opportunities as you or have the ability to travel or comprehend your culture. Learning about your new friend's personality and cultural norms will help avert heartbreaks. (Does he or she easily fall in love? Is he or she looking for an opportunity to leave the country?)

Having a relationship during your adventure can be as exhilarating as the trip itself, yet it does have its pitfalls. Erin discovered for herself the ups and downs of such an interaction while traveling. "It was exciting to meet someone from another country. We got really close, really fast. I saw it as an opportunity to go live in England for three months and be with someone I really liked. But, unless you're both really willing to make sacrifices, it's really hard to make that work."

Jeannette's Advice

What do you need to know about love, romance, sex, and travel before you go? Here are several points to think about:

1. You are most likely to have a fling with a fellow traveler. One woman I know spent a romantic time with a Parisian photographer she encountered in Bangkok.

2. A foreign lover can be your ticket to seeing everyday life in a foreign culture. In places with tourist enclaves—think resort areas of the Caribbean—a local boyfriend can be one avenue, and perhaps the easiest way, to get to really know a place.

3. Ethics and etiquette for the female traveler often boil down to the same rules you really should be following at home. Avoid temptation if you are happily married. Treat your lover as a flesh-and-blood man, without condescending to him if he is younger and poorer, or leading him on if this is just a fling for you. Surprising as it may seem, often the man is the one who can get hurt, especially if he lives in Oceania or the Middle East, where sincere men may lose their hearts to a female traveler they have no means to ever see again.

4. Let coffee or tea be your drink of seduction, not alcohol. You need to have your radar fully operating to detect whether danger—or merely mutually satisfactory amusement—are on a foreign guy's mind.

15.

REACH OUT AND
TOUCH SOMEONE

S IMPLY *having the ability to communicate
with friends and family can provide you
with a bit of comfort while traveling, particularly on a longer trip, even if you never take
advantage of emailing, phoning, or writing.*

❧ Before You Leave

It's important to have established ways of communicating with those at home in the event of an emergency. Prior to hitting the road, provide your family and close friends with your itinerary, the phone numbers of where you'll be staying, contact info for anyone you'll be visiting along the way, and an email address that you'll be logging in to en route.

If you're traveling for an extended period of time and fear that your friends will worry if you don't return their phone calls in a timely manner, send them a short email giving them a heads-up that you'll be on the road. Bear in mind that changing your cell phone or home phone's voice-mail message to indicate that you're away may alert a burglar that your home is empty.

Set your work email to an auto response so that anyone trying to contact you will know that your response may be delayed. Put your business commitments on hold and have someone else handle any potential issues that may arise. Provide a co-worker with an email address to contact you with any emergencies. This will keep you removed from the day-to-day issues of work. If you have someone house-sitting, handling your bills, or taking care of pets, give them the same information, so you can be easily contacted for any issues at home.

❧ Email

I suggest that you use this easy and cheap method of communication with restraint. Internet cafés are abundant and, while they are a great way to meet other travelers who are also checking their email, staying in too close of contact with friends and family back home could hinder you from immersing yourself in your journey and the local culture.

Stefany traveled to New Zealand for a month while her husband was at home. "I didn't spend that much time emailing. I'd let family know that they wouldn't hear from me for a week or 10 days, and then it was really exciting when I went to check my email."

Rather than emailing, you may wish to create a blog to keep family and friends updated on your whereabouts. They can view the blog at their convenience to read about your trip, and post comments back to you. Keeping a blog will allow you to document your journey as you would in a diary through words and photos, and share it with others in real time. To create your own free blog, try Travel Blogs (www.travelblogs.com), Blogger (www.blogger.com), or TravelPod (www.travelpod.com).

Blogs are very easy to create and maintain through one of these sites. Consider setting it up prior to your departure, so that you won't be learning the finer points of blogging while you're on the road.

✿ Phone

Cell Phones—You may be able to travel outside your country and use your current cell phone if it is equipped with Global System for Mobile Communications (GSM). This digital technology transfers mobile voice and data services and is available in more than 200 countries. If you plan to travel internationally and need or wish to make and receive calls, confirm whether the country to which you are traveling utilizes GSM through the GSM World website (www.gsmworld.com). Then find out if your cell phone's manufacturer utilizes the technology. Finally, make sure it won't cost you an arm and a leg if you use it. Your service provider can provide you with per-minute costs.

Consider purchasing a SIM card once you arrive at your destination. These cards are placed in your cell phone and connect you with the local network. There will be a charge for the card itself and you may have to purchase a specified number of minutes. But, this could be the cheapest (though not always the most convenient if you can't find a store that sells the cards) way to phone both in-country and out.

Rather than using your current cell phone, purchasing a prepaid mobile phone prior to departure or at your destination may be more economical and useful if you'll be making hotel and dinner reservations on the fly. Starting at about USD $50, Mobal (www.mobal.com) allows you to purchase a GSM-equipped phone and then pay for minutes (by credit card only) when you use the phone. There's no monthly charge, and you only pay for what you use. In most cases, rates are higher than if you were to use a phone card, but you can't beat the convenience for making reservations at a moment's notice. Mobal has two versions of phones; only the more-expensive one will work when calling from North America.

Hot Tip! If you carry a cell phone, save your hotel's phone number on it, as well as any other travel-related numbers (such as your airline) that you may need while traveling.

Phone Cards—Phone cards are a handy alternative to carrying a phone. Some cards available in North America can connect you to foreign countries, as well as from other countries to North America. Shop around, as rates vary tremendously. Costco sells a card that charges just 3.5 cents per minute in the United States and has excellent rates to foreign countries. Your phone-service provider may also offer a card for use abroad.

The Case for Phone Cards

While traveling through Greece, I didn't have a specific itinerary for where I wanted to go. I only had a general idea of a couple of islands I was interested in visiting. Without advance reservations for hotels, I found that using a phone card was the perfect way to communicate not only within the country, but also for calling home to the United States.

I easily purchased the card at a small shop. It was the size of a credit card, and had a beautiful drawing on it that was typical of Greece. I never did use up the entire card, but when I returned home I continued to use it for a bookmark until I passed it along to a friend traveling to Athens.—BW

With the explosion of cell-phone use, the number of telephone booths is diminishing. Best bets for finding them include post offices, rest areas, gas stations, and convenience stores. You can also use a phone card with the telephone in your hotel room. If necessary, you may even be able to use a phone card at a small restaurant or shop where the kind owner gives you permission.

Skype — I first used Skype (www.skype.com) while I was traveling solo in India. I was a bit homesick and lonely for my very significant other, Jon, back at home. I popped into an Internet café where the computers were equipped with Skype. I simply logged on and voila—I was connected with Jon via a web camera.

I was self-conscious about having a full-on conversation with him since there were others in the café, but Skype allowed us to instant message and see each other at the same time. I was even able to move the portable camera around enough to show him street scenes in Kolkata.

Skype is a voice-over-Internet service that you simply download onto your computer. As long as the person you're speaking with also has an account, it's free. You can also pay to call regular landlines and cell phones via Skype. With a microphone and headset combination, you can communicate with others across the world and, if there's a webcam connected to the computer, you can actually see each other as well.

Text Messaging—Text messaging is merely the sending of a brief message from one cell phone to another. Sending these is far more popular in other countries than it is in North America. It is more economical than making a phone call, and is a quick and easy way to stay in touch with friends and family members, especially when there is a big time difference between you and your loved ones.

Check with your cell phone company for charges on incoming and outgoing messages as the difference can vary greatly. AT&T once quoted me 50 cents for sending and 15 cents for receiving messages in India.

In-Room Phones—Some hotels in North America will allow you to make free local calls from the phone in your room, while others will charge you a dollar or more per call—even if you're calling a toll-free number. Outside of North America, hotels charge on a per-call basis. Know what your hotel charges before dialing. It might make more sense to use your own cell phone or a calling card.

Mail

Postcards—Remember these? A handwritten postcard or letter is a welcome addition to anyone's mailbox. Your friends who receive a unique postcard will feel special. And when you write them, you'll feel connected to those poor souls who are schlepping away at work while you're out blazing trails on the Annapurna trek or swimming with dolphins in New Zealand.

Postcards can help you thoughtfully document your trip, and they give you something to do when you dine alone or when you just want to hibernate in your room . . . and it's fun to shop for postcards or stationery from local stores.

Hot Tip! Before your trip, print names and addresses on mailing labels. When you write a postcard, using a label will allow you to keep track of whom you've already written.

Post Restante—You can receive mail abroad by having letters or packages sent to a general-delivery address at any post office, although post offices in major cities will be far more reliable than those in rural locations. Let your loved ones know approximately where in the world you'll be and when. Have them write your name prominently on the envelope or box, followed by the words "Post Restante" on the second line, then the post office's address. You may be charged a small per-piece fee.

If the postal clerk can't find mail you're expecting, have him or her look for mail under your first name, in case it's misfiled.

Leslie had a unique use for the postal system during her adventures. "I really missed my Sunday morning routine after I'd been traveling through Europe for two months, so I had my boyfriend mail me my favorite sections of the Sunday paper."

16.

HURDLING LANGUAGE BARRIERS

ALTHOUGH *not knowing a given language is a popular excuse for not traveling beyond your own border, you don't need to be fluent to have a rewarding and fun adventure. As a matter of fact, learning the language can be an adventure in itself! It's easier than you think to learn a few basic words, and you'll win over the locals for your efforts.*

✤ Learn a Few Phrases

Not only is it respectful to learn at least a few local phrases when you're traveling to another country, but it'll make the trip more fun and interesting. To begin with, the basics are fine and learning the following words and phrases will take you a long way with the locals:

Hello	Excuse me.
My name is . . .	I'm sorry.
What is your name?	Where is . . . ?
Do you speak English?	How do you say this in
Goodbye	(insert language)?
Please	How much is this?
Thank you	That's too much!
Yes	I like . . .
No	

Your guidebook, a foreign phrase book or dictionary, a language program, or the Internet are all good resources for picking up these phrases; you can write them out on a cheat sheet prior to arriving in each country.

In addition to the basics, if you have special dietary requirements or allergies, you'll want to include words for these in your language repertoire. As a vegetarian, I know firsthand how important it is to explain what I can and can't eat. Some lessons come only with experience, however. I learned after eating a few bowlfuls of soup during one trip that chicken is not considered meat in Vietnam. Well, at least not meat as in *thit*, which my guidebook translates as "meat." *Khong thit* (no meat), means that you might or might not have chicken added.

Alison had no trouble finding English speakers during her backpacking trip through Europe. Even so, she said "I learned enough in the local language to not order horsemeat from the menu."

Tonal languages such as Chinese and Thai are extremely difficult to learn, but you can bet the locals will be that much more appreciative if you give it a try! It can be embarrassing and intimidating with any language because you're sure to make mistakes and some will laugh at you . . . but so what?

Have fun!

Laura hasn't had any problems with language barriers in her travels. She lumps language issues into two categories: "There's one barrier to get through in order to take care of yourself. This one's easy because people are trying to sell you a room or food, although you may be surprised at what you ordered. The second category, rudimentary conversations, is always the same. (What's your name? Where are you from? . . .) I wish I knew enough of the language so I could talk about what I've read or something going on in the world."

Even if you can't get beyond the easy conversation, locals will appreciate your attempt to speak their language, and after a couple of brief phrases you may find that their English is better than they initially let on. It's common for those in non-English-speaking countries to hold back, as they may feel self-conscious if they don't speak "perfect" English. After polite greetings, it's perfectly fine to ask them, in their language, whether they speak English. It will still benefit you to try to continue the conversation in their language when possible.

There are several ways to learn a language, whether you want to learn just the basics or are more serious about it. Your options will depend on the amount of time and money you have to dedicate to the process.

❦ Audio Programs

Audio programs, the least-expensive way to learn phrases, introduce you to a language and allow you to listen to correct pronunciation. Downloads are available from iTunes and Audible, or you can pick up language-learning programs on CDs. Courses that include a few CDs for less than USD $20 will get you started. You can also borrow or download programs from your local library. The greatest benefit to these courses is that you can listen to them wherever and whenever you like. I find that audio programs suit me best because I can commute around town and brush up on my Spanish at the same time by listening to CDs in my car. I have to watch out though. While driving, I've been so caught up on listening and pronouncing that I've missed my exit more than once!

❦ Take a Class

You can also learn a language by taking an evening class in traveler's lingo at a community college, university, or community center in your area. While it will set you back a few more dollars than a purchased audio program, sometimes it takes a financial commitment and regular time investment before you'll throw yourself into the process. You may find that the interaction with the class and the opportunity to ask questions better suits your needs.

❦ Study Abroad

Many people study a language by taking classes abroad while spending an extended amount of time in one location. Programs may even offer you the chance to live with a non- English-speaking family so that you experience complete immersion.

Choose your program based on what language you want to learn, and then choose where you'd like to spend time. Bear in mind that for some languages, you can learn it in more than one country: Spanish is spoken in Mexico or Spain, for instance. Search online for programs that suit your needs. Languages Abroad (www.languagesabroad.com), which offers programs in 30 languages and in 50 countries, is among the many choices of study-abroad options.

Make it Simple

When you're speaking in English to non-native English speakers, use simple words and speak slowly (not loudly). A non-native English speaker will more easily understand you if you use the same kind of basic words you learn when studying a language. If he or she doesn't understand you the first time, try again by using simpler words and enunciating clearly.

I had been doing this for years without realizing it, until I met my friend's parents, who were visiting from India. While their English was very good, I found myself rephrasing sentences when they didn't quite understand either my English or my accent. They later mentioned how easy it was to communicate with me. I realized that my experience over the years with non-native English speakers made it second nature for me to translate my own sentences into simpler words.

Hire an Interpreter

To learn more about the local people and culture, consider hiring a guide or interpreter who can help translate and explain the customs, environment, architecture, and anything else that might interest you. Before your trip, check with the embassy of the country you're planning to visit, or check online for guides at your destination. Once you arrive, check with tourist offices, tour companies, or your own embassy.

Always ask for references, and try to meet the guide before you secure his or her services. Be sure to choose someone you're confident can speak English, as well as the language spoken by the people or area you'll be visiting.

I once hired a guide in a remote village in Northern Thailand. While the guide was Thai, the village was inhabited by long-neck women from the Karen tribe, originally from Myanmar. These beautiful (but some say repressed) women wore multiple rings of brass around their necks, ultimately atrophying their neck muscles. The guide could not speak their language, and I felt like I was at a zoo observing an exotic group of people with whom I couldn't communicate.

Locals are often willing to accompany you as a guide so they can practice their English. For the price of a meal or a small gift, you may find someone who will open up a world of insight into the local culture. You may even be invited to their home for dinner. Assess the situation, and if you feel it's safe, take them up on the offer. Their families may be eager to practice English, and you'll get a peek into an authentic local lifestyle.

If you're traveling on business, an interpreter or guide is necessary. You won't want to skimp on this, as a skilled guide will be invaluable at helping you interpret not only the language, but social cues. Your own employer or the clients or customers you're visiting might be able to connect you with someone who is experienced and a specialist in your industry.

Use Visual Aids and Hand Gestures

Phrasebooks and pocket dictionaries are a handy reference when you're on the road. They can refresh your memory from the language-learning you did before your trip and will allow you to look up words as you chat with the locals. If you're going to a country where the script is non-Roman (Chinese or Thai, for example), your phrasebook should include English, the local script, and a phonetic spelling.

Keep a notebook or a sheet of paper with common phrases and words, or write them in the front cover of your phrasebook and carry it with you at all times.

A laminated, passport-sized folding card from Kwikpoint (www.kwikpoint.com) allows you to say it with pictures. It includes more than 600 internationally recognized drawings for easily getting across your message.

Of course, in a pinch, hand gestures and body language can often get you through most situations. While traveling in France, Erin found that, "You get thrown into situations where you have to be expressive. If you know just enough of the language, you can muddle through by miming."

Marion travels the world to buy fabric for her business, Safekeeper Vest (www.safekeepervest.com). She creates vests for travelers with lots of great "secret" pockets to keep your items safe. As Marion bounces from India to Japan to France, the fact that she doesn't speak another language never hinders her from finding the quality fabric that she requires. "I enjoy the experiences I've had with merchants, and the fact that I can communicate so well with them," she says. "I convey what I want by wearing a Safekeeper vest and showing them what I'm looking for. My nose leads me to the right places, and I can find the good cloth in about two days. I have to be a good bargainer because the things I want are not common. I speak my language and they speak their language, and we figure out a common ground. It's never held me back from getting what I'm after."

Laugh and Have Fun

People in some cultures will let you stumble through their language and laugh along with you. They might gently correct and tease you until you get it right. Sometimes you'll find yourself

Lost in Translation

I took a taxi in Hanoi and asked the driver to take me to the Hanoi Opera Hotel, which is a huge landmark in the city. My much smaller hotel was nearby, and I knew that if I could get a taxi driver to drop me off at the Hanoi Opera Hotel, I could then walk to my far humbler lodging.

Driving over railroad tracks that I knew were leading in the opposite direction, I repeated "Opera Hotel." "Yes, yes, Obaga," the taxi driver said. When he didn't turn the taxi around, I once again reiterated my destination and he replied with "Obaga." I questioned myself and wondered if he knew a back way to the hotel that I wasn't aware of.

While I was never afraid for my safety, I became convinced that we were headed in the wrong direction and insisted he turn around. Finally, I was able to point him to the large hotel. "See? Opera Hotel," I said emphatically and a bit perturbed. In very good English, he said, "Oh, Hanoi Opera Hotel." Somehow, something definitely got lost in translation. We were speaking the same language with accents different enough to send us in opposite directions. Six years later, I still chuckle to myself every time I hear the word "opera." And I learned to always carry the address of my hotel with me.—BW

giving it your best effort, perhaps completing a full sentence in Portuguese to order your black coffee with milk, only to find that the waiter replies to you in English (a minor blessing).

If you don't take yourself too seriously, communicating (or miscommunicating) can be laughter filled, and you may find that you make a few friends in the process.

17.

RESPONSIBLE TRAVEL

TOURISM *is intrusive by its very nature. When traveling, you will be interacting with locals and their environment. How you conduct yourself and the impression you leave behind will affect residents, even in the most subtle of ways. And the more remote a region and its people, the greater potential of having an impact. Make your contribution to the world positive by incorporating low-impact habits when encountering locals and spending time in their surroundings.*

🍃 Culture Shock

When you're traveling in a place that's far from familiar, it's common to feel disoriented or overwhelmed by new sights and sounds. The disorientation, confusion, and misunderstandings that are a part of travel can be lessened if you have an open mind and know what you will be experiencing in advance, so there are fewer surprises.

🍃 Learn Local Customs

Finding the locals staring at you or, worse, acting belligerently because you are unwittingly committing a cultural faux pas, can be embarrassing. Did you know it's not proper to stab your food with chopsticks when in Asia? Or that you should never take pictures of Maya Indians in Guatemala without their permission?

Read up on your destination before you go so you're not caught making such blunders, which constitute disrespectful behavior. Start by reading either the Culture Smart! or Culture Shock! guides. Both provide in-depth information on countries and cities, and include background information from history, to religion, to politics. They also include details on dealing with and understanding the culture, including hand gestures, fitting in with the locals, and making friends.

For more in-depth information, see the guidebook publishers listed in Chapter 4, Mapping Out the Details, and search for books at your local independent bookstore, at the library, or online.

A broad search on the Internet will provide you with an abundance of information. Wikitravel (wikitravel.org) and the CIA World Factbook are comprehensive online resources offering information to help you better understand a culture.

Wikitravel provides information about culture, politics, and history for every country and city you could possibly visit, and it links to tourism offices, interactive maps, and even suggested movies about a given area. This site is built with community effort so, on occasion, information will be incorrect—take it with a grain of salt. While their website design leaves a lot to be desired, the CIA World Factbook is an excellent resource for facts and figures on countries. It's rather dry (surprised?), but it's informative.

Even though I read up on another culture prior to my trip, I find that I don't fully "get" a particular cultural habit until I'm there. Having advance knowledge, however, helps me assimilate and not be shocked by what is considered normal behavior by the locals.

Once you arrive, watch the locals for cues in terms of appropriate conduct. Tricia spent two years in the Peace Corps in Bolivia. Her travel experience has given her the confidence to be patient. While some travelers might want to take control of a situation that's unfamiliar to them, she says, "I'm aware that I don't know everything. I sit back and watch the locals in order to fit in." And when she does ask for help, what does she do? She asks a woman.

Sue, who travels to rural areas around the United States to discover music, has found a way to engage with the locals in her own country. "Don't pretend that you belong there, but show respect for what would actually interest them by asking lots of questions."

❧ Cultures

While the rise in tourism over the last half century has certainly brought the world together and increased our understanding

Cultural Respect

I lived in Sydney, Australia, for a few months in the early 90s, and for much of that time, I crashed in a large apartment with a group of musicians. Their band included an Australian aborigine and a rather large Maori chief. We lived in Redfern, which was renowned for its population of aborigines. They came from the desert, where it's traditional to spend the evening around a fire pit, telling stories of the dreamtime, and playing the didgeridoo. These were not city folk, and it was an economically depressed area.

You would think that a short blond "yank" would be intimidated and hassled in this neighborhood. On the contrary, my neighbors were quite nice to me. A nod and "How ya goin', mate," from me seemed to endear them. I truly believe that by showing them respect and not judging them for their living conditions, they returned the favor and were just as intrigued by this gutsy white gal.—BW

of both cultures abroad and immigrants in our own neighborhood, the effect has brought its share of problems.

Native cultures and traditional events and festivals are becoming watered down by strong Western influences, including the influx of tourists and U.S. brand-name products. In many developing countries, locals have come to expect and anticipate support from tourists through small amounts of money and gifts given to children. Even in the most remote areas of Nepal, it's not uncommon to be accosted by children begging for money and pencils.

Amy learned a thing or two about begging after six months in India. "It's sad if an 8-year-old girl knocks on your car window and starts dancing when you're stopped in the street. It's sad because the whole family is making the girl go out there to dance. It's a tragic situation. If you give her money, you're feeding into the cycle." Ultimately, this encourages other adults to do the same with their children.

She continues, "It's hard to know what the right thing to do is. Do your cultural research in the guidebooks and do what you can to be gracious, good, and thoughtful."

Not only are cultures changing due to tourism, but indigenous languages are being lost. According to UNESCO (www.unesco.org), one language is lost every two weeks, and half of the world's 6,000 languages are endangered. This is occurring, in part, because communities must adopt more popular languages in order to attain economic stability.

As an example, the ability of the Mien hill tribe of northern Thailand to trade, sell goods, and build businesses increases dramatically if they can communicate with other Thai people, as well as tourists. The tribe benefits by speaking Thai or even English, rather than their own language, Miao-Yao. However, in adapting, the loss of their language is the first step in the loss of their culture.

Chris from Crooked Trails, which develops and leads tours that help sustain local communities without a dramatic impact to their culture. "We show the people we're visiting how tourism can be friendly and that they have a say in what's going on. If we can provide some kind of economic benefit to the community, then perhaps the kids won't be racing to the cities and leaving their homes. They then see value in their own culture."

A hot debate rages over whether to travel to countries where human rights are woefully ignored, such as North Korea and Myanmar. An argument can be made on one side that traveling

17. RESPONSIBLE TRAVEL

to these countries will help break down social barriers and will help the locals become more progressive by exposing them to Western ideas. On the other hand, some believe that traveling to countries where the locals are suppressed only helps to fund the government through tourist dollars. Aung San Suu Kyi, the pro-democracy leader of Myanmar who has remained under house arrest for the majority of time since 1989, recommends that travelers not go to her country. To learn about human rights in the countries to which you may be planning to travel, check out Amnesty International's website (www.amnesty.org).

It's easier for solo travelers to have a low-impact experience with regards to the culture of a place. Large groups can be intimidating to the locals, and when you're on your own, you will have more opportunity for one-on-one encounters. As a result, you'll be able to break down barriers and preconceived notions others may have about your own country, and learn more about the country you're visiting. As Diane Redfern, publisher of Connecting: Solo Travel Network (www.cstn.org) explains, "When you're traveling on your own and people approach you, animosity toward your government disappears."

Even the smallest of gestures has an impact. You can start by doing the following to make a positive impression:

- Learn some of the language, blend in, and do not act raucously.

- Create positive experiences by simply being nice and respectful; act as an ambassador of your country.

- Help out the locals by volunteering on a project.

- Buy crafts handmade by the locals, frequent independently owned shops.

- When you return home, raise awareness about the political and social environments of countries you've visited. Talk to your friends and co-workers, attend events, and support organizations that are in line with your philosophies.
- Be respectful of local religious customs.

☙ Environment

In addition to the effects that tourism has on indigenous cultures, the environment is suffering, as well.

Communities rely on local resources to provide tourists with both basic necessities and luxury items. In developing countries, this often means that the environment is being stripped of natural resources, such as water and wood. In the short term, locals may not have enough of a natural resource for themselves. In the long term, it affects the biodiversity within a country; two examples are the rainforests of Brazil, where logging is decimating the area, and the Great Barrier Reef in Australia, where polluted runoff from nearby wastewater systems, overuse, and global warming are killing the coral reef.

Recreational activities such as jet skiing (which generates noise and water pollution), scuba diving (in which careless divers can disturb marine life and damage ecosystems such as reefs), and trekking (in which garbage is often left behind in remote villages) can have hazardous impacts on the environment. In addition, the strain caused by overusage of electricity and water to accommodate the increase in tourism has a strong effect on local environments. There's much concern in countries such as Costa Rica, where communities are unable to support the rapid influx of tourists because they have little in the way of sewage and water-treatment infrastructure.

17. RESPONSIBLE TRAVEL

ᴥᴥᴥ Brenda's Story ᴥᴥᴥ

While guiding a group on a photography workshop, we went to a traditional camel market in Egypt. Other tour groups had visited this market, so the locals knew what to expect. We had to buy tickets to enter and photograph in the market, and we then had the freedom to photograph throughout the area. However, it was a courtesy to ask permission if we photographed people who were outside of the market.

I saw four guys sitting off to the side who were shepherds at a holding corral for the camels. I held up my camera and started to take pictures. One of the guys motioned with his hand, but I didn't know what he was doing. He did it again, and I finally realized that I was standing above them while they were sitting down. In essence, I was towering above them as if I was the one in control of the situation.

When I finally understood what was happening, I crouched down to shoot, and actually ended up getting a better picture. At that point, they all lit up.

If you want to get the best photos, you'll want to blend in as much as possible. As an American, you will stand out in foreign countries, but you don't want to be outrageous in your dress, and you'll want to learn what the proper protocols are for any given culture. I recommend that people learn as much as possible about the culture in advance.

Water is becoming an ever-more-precious resource. Many hotels now suggest that you leave towels on the floor if you want them washed; otherwise, they expect you to reuse them. This saves a tremendous amount of water. And many restaurants will only serve water at your request. Movements worldwide have begun to counteract the effects of tourism on cultures and environment.

Hot Tip! If your lodging doesn't have a policy allowing you to re-use towels and bedding to save water, you can make this happen by keeping the "Do Not Disturb" sign on your door, so the towels and bedding will not be changed.

Ecotourism—Ecotourism promotes environmental sustainability and responsibility in travel to natural areas. It encourages travelers to minimize their impact by promoting recycling, as well as water and energy conservation. By helping to preserve the environment, you're also improving the general well-being of the locals. When responsible tourism can be implemented, the indigenous population is more likely to remain in their village or region rather than fleeing to cities, where jobs may be more plentiful.

If you are not used to recycling, conserving water, or generally being gentle on the environment, I urge you to take this opportunity to incorporate some Earth-friendly habits into your life. Even innocently leaving water running in a sink for a short period of time can have a harmful effect on an area with water shortages. Some communities in North America have recently been forced to shut down their businesses for short periods of time in the summer due to water scarcity.

Independent travelers are faced with opportunities every day to slow down the progress of environmental erosion. To do your part, please consider the following:

- Carry water-filtration tablets, a filter, or water purifier rather than buying bottled water.

- Clean up your garbage. Never leave it behind—especially if you're backpacking or hiking. And recycle whenever possible.

17. RESPONSIBLE TRAVEL

215

- Reuse towels and bedding at hotels to save on water consumption.

- Turn off the water while brushing your teeth, and take short showers instead of a bath.

- Choose fresh, locally grown foods over imported foods.

- When offered a choice, opt for non-mechanized recreation: Nordic skiing instead of snowmobiling, sailing instead of jet skiing.

- Whenever possible, take a form of transportation that causes the least amount of pollution (a cyclo over a motorbike, public transportation over a taxi).

- Utilize a carbon buy-back program to lessen the impact of your flight by offsetting the harmful emissions. Try TerraPass (www.terrapass.com) or search online for other popular programs.

- If on a wildlife tour, do not disturb (or feed) wild animals; stay at least 200 feet from whales and other sea life.

- Don't buy products made from endangered animals or plants.

- Stay on maintained trails when hiking.

♪♪♪ Meg's Story ♪♪♪

While on a tenting safari in Kenya, our small group sat around a campfire with Maasai warriors who had been hired to guard us in the game park. While it was great to get the two groups together (Westerners and Kenyans), the Maasai were distinctly uncomfortable that first night and didn't participate in the storytelling I had suggested—one story from Kenya, one from Sweden, one from America.

On the second night, three warriors appeared, probably because the first two wanted to show their buddy the strange Westerners who insisted that we all sit together around the fire. They spoke no English to us, but by the end of that evening, after they had heard themselves on my small tape recorder, they were all smiles and insisted on singing four songs with innumerable verses.

The rhythms were complicated and the head movements and repetitive clicking noises fascinated me. Moffat Wachera, our guide, translated the lyrics for us: tales of bravery, usually ending with the dramatic slaying of a lion. There was a definite camaraderie by the end of the evening, and I stayed and watched the cook stir flour into boiling water to make ugali, which we all sampled. (I'll try anything once.) Goodnights were cordial, signified by smiles and bowing, hands together in prayer-like fashion.

My fondest memory of those two evenings was the contrast between the initial aloofness of the men and the joy with which they ultimately accepted our offer of friendship. As I zipped up my tent, I could see the Maasai silently standing guard and swaying gently as if to their inner music, happy, I was sure, that their stories were heard and appreciated.

17. RESPONSIBLE TRAVEL

18.

COMING HOME

I tend to get culture shock when I return home from a trip. Reverse culture shock. It's that shake-my-head-with-astonishment feeling when I walk into a grocery store and see the overwhelming number of choices I'm faced with. I wonder aloud why there's an entire aisle of soda and another aisle of chips. I stare into my closet full of clothes, wondering why I have so many pairs of jeans when I'm really most fond of two. I know I'm over my reverse culture shock when I start complaining that I have nothing to wear and there's nothing good to eat. To help ease yourself back into life at home, following are some thoughts and suggestions.

Logistics

Logistically and emotionally, it helps to have made your arrival arrangements in advance. Have a good friend pick you up at the airport. Provide her with all of your flight details in case your plane is delayed. Have a backup plan (the phone number of the local shuttle will do) in case she gets stuck at work. Carry your cell phone with you (even if you never use it on your trip) so that you can easily make calls for these arrangements when you arrive at the airport, train, or bus terminal.

Clean and tidy up your home before your departure. When you return, it will help ease you back into life at home. For me, there's nothing worse than coming home to a sink full of dishes. If you have a house-sitter, let her know your expectation for a clean place when you return.

Post-trip Depression

Post-trip depression is common upon returning home from an adventure, as we settle back into the doldrums of everyday life, with dishes, bills, phone calls, and email. It's common to feel mired in the details of work and home, and to miss the sun, fun, or food from your travels.

There are ways to stretch your vacation in order to ease you back to "normal" life.

Don't plan on cooking your first night back. On your way home from the airport, swing by the supermarket for healthful prepared foods, or find a restaurant that can serve up a special meal. If you're like me, you'll want to hold onto your vacation by having a meal similar to what you would be eating if still on your trip. Quesadillas? Greek salad? Squid skewers? Or perhaps you've been craving comfort food, fresh fish, a milkshake, or pizza. Either way, budget this extra expense into your travel fund before you go, as it will help you adjust to everyday life.

Hot Tip! Pad your trip with an extra day at home so that you aren't returning in the evening and going back to work the next morning. Ease back into your lifestyle.

Make arrangements as soon as you get back to have coffee or dinner with people who have traveled and are eager to hear your stories and see your photos (extending the same courtesy and enthusiasm when they return from a trip). Upload photos to an online photo sharing site and share them with family and friends.

Plan to spend some time poring over your pictures, souvenirs, and other items you've collected along the way (such as ticket stubs and coins), and consider putting together a scrapbook. Stay connected with your journey and try not to switch back into your "other" life too abruptly. You'll eventually get settled in anyway; no need to rush it.

If you find yourself dealing with reverse culture shock, there are a few things you can do to get through it.

- Avoid large chain stores and restaurants. Instead, frequent independently owned shops and support the locals, just as you hopefully did while traveling.

- Keep the television turned off. Stay away from the news on the radio and in newspapers.

- Eat well; don't eat unhealthy food in response to your sadness about being home.

18. COMING HOME

- Take long nature walks, perhaps with a friend who is eager to hear about your travels.

As you ease back into life, most importantly, appreciate what you have and where you are, but start saving immediately for that next adventure!

19.

ONE LAST WORD

Traveling has sent me on a trajectory course that I could not have imagined more than 20 years ago. And in retrospect, I cannot imagine who I would be without having discovered the world of travel. Yes, solo women adventurers forged paths before me, but I was (and still am) considered the black sheep in my family for pursuing my passion and am an anomaly among my oldest and dearest friends.

You may find that your desire for travel isn't shared by your family and peers. However, don't allow anything, whether self-doubts or outside influences, to stop you from exploring this extraordinary world we live in.

It has never been easier for travelers in general, and women specifically, to venture around the world, as we have access to information about every possible destination (the Internet), an inexpensive way to communicate with family and friends at home (email) and access to technologies that provide us with a safety net if we need help (cell phones).

My hundreds of thousands of miles of globe trotting have exposed me to a world filled with wonder and awe-inspiring moments. It's a world of good, in which strangers do not hesitate to help when they see someone who's lost or in need. You can trust that when you are on the road, you will be the recipient of kindness, and you will, in turn, have opportunities to reach out to others. You can also trust that every day will be more exciting and marvelous than the previous.

It doesn't have to be a round-the-world trip or a 7,000-mile motorcycle journey, but whatever your dreams are, start planning that adventure today. Once you allow your dreams to see the light of day, I guarantee you will find strengths you didn't know you had, and your travels will impact your life in countless positive ways once you return home.

In the words of Eleanor Roosevelt, "You must do the thing you think you cannot do." Shifting your attitude to a belief that you can indeed accomplish anything will be the first step of your journey.

Travel Well!

Beth

WEBSITE RESOURCES

Accessible Journeys	www.disabilitytravel.com
Access-Able Travel Source	www.access-able.com
Action for Southern Africa	www.actsa.org
Adventure Cycling Association	www.adventurecycling.org
Airborne	www.airbornehealth.com
Amateur Traveler	www.amateurtraveler.com
Amazon.com	www.amazon.com
American Automobile Association	www.aaa.com
American Express	www.americanexpress.com
American Hiking Society	www.americanhiking.org
Ames Walker	www.ameswalker.com
Amnesty International	www.amnesty.org
Ancestry.com	www.ancestry.com
Arthur Frommer's Budget Travel	www.budgettravelonline.com
Athletic-Minded Traveler	www.athleticmindedtraveler.com
Audible.com	www.audible.com
Beau Wine Tours and Limousine Service	www.beauwinetours.com
Better Business Bureau	www.bbb.org
Bike Friday	www.bikefriday.com
Blogger	www.blogger.com
Bose	www.bose.com
Brenda Tharp Photography	www.brendatharp.com
Bureau of Transportation Statistics	www.bts.gov
Canadian Automobile Association	www.caa.ca
Centers for Disease Control	www.cdc.gov
Chowhound	www.chowhound.com

CIA's World Factbook	www.cia.gov/cia/publications/factbook
Citysearch	www.citysearch.com
CNET Networks	www.cnet.com
Coastline Travel Advisors	www.coastlinetravel.com
Columbia Sportswear Company	www.columbia.com
Connecting: Solo Travel Network	www.cstn.org
Coolibar	www.coolibar.com
CouchSurfing	www.couchsurfing.com
Craigslist	www.craigslist.org
CrateWorks	www.crateworks.com
Crooked Trails	www.crookedtrails.com
Cross-Cultural Solutions	www.crossculturalsolutions.org
Disabled Travelers Guide to the World	www.disabledtravelersguide.com
DisabledTravelers.com	www.disabledtravelers.com
DivaCup	www.divacup.com
Dorling Kindersley	www.dk.com
DuVine Adventures	www.duvine.com
Eagle Creek	www.eaglecreek.com
Earth Calendar	www.earthcalendar.net
Earthwatch Institute	www.earthwatch.org
Eat Smart Guides	www.eatsmartguides.com
Edwards Luggage	www.edwardsluggage.com
Elderhostel	www.elderhostel.org
Eurail	www.eurail.com
European Ramblers' Association	www.era-ewv-ferp.org
ExOfficio	www.exofficio.com
Expedia	www.expedia.com
Farecast	www.farecast.com
Festivals.com	www.festivals.com
Flickr	www.flickr.com
Garmin	www.garmin.com
Geocaching.com	www.geocaching.com

GlobalFreeloaders	www.globalfreeloaders.com
Global Refund	www.globalrefund.com
Global Volunteers	www.globalvolunteers.org
Globe Riders	www.globeriders.com
Google Maps	www.maps.google.com
Green Theme International Home Exchange	www.gti-home-exchange.com
GSM World	www.gsmworld.com
Habitat for Humanity International	www.habitat.org
HomeExchange.com	www.homeexchange.com
Hostelling International	www.hihostels.com
Iberian Moto Tours	www.imtbike.com
iExplore	www.iexplore.com
iJourneys	www.ijourneys.com
Indie Travel Podcast	www.indietravelpodcast.com
Injinji	www.injinji.com
Insure My Trip	www.insuremytrip.com
International Air Transport Association	www.iata.org
International Association of Medical Assistance	www.iamat.org
Intervac Home Exchange	www.intervacus.com
iTunes	www.apple.com /itunes
JetBlue Airways	www.jetblue.com
Kayak	www.kayak.com
Kiss-Off	www.kissoff.com
Kodak Gallery	www.kodakgallery.com
Kwikpoint	www.kwikpoint.com
Languages Abroad	www.languagesabroad.com
Lastminute.com	www.lastminute.com
Lonely Planet	www.lonelyplanet.com
Magellan's Travel Supplies	www.magellans.com
Mapquest Mobile	www.mapquest.com /mobile

MEDEX	www.medexassist.com
MedicAlert	www.medicalert.com
MedicalSummary	www.medicalsummary.com
Medjet Assist	www.medjetassistance.com
Michelin Guides	www.viamichelin.com
Mobal	www.mobal.com
Moki Treks	www.mokitreks.com
MotoDiscovery	www.motodiscovery.com
MyPublisher	www.mypublisher.com
National Geographic Adventure	www. adventure. nationalgeographic.com/
Netflix	www.netflix.com
New Orleans Culinary History Tours	www.noculinarytours.com
No-Jet-Lag	www.nojetlag.com
Northwest Airlines	www.nwa.com
OneDerWear	www.onederwear.com
Orbitz	www.orbitz.com
Pacsafe	www.pacsafe.com
Passport Canada	www.ppt.gc.ca
Priority Pass	www.prioritypass.com
RailPass	www.railpass.com
Recreational Equipment, Inc.	www.rei.com
Rick Steves' Europe Through the Back Door	www.ricksteves.com
Roadfood	www.roadfood.com
RootsWeb.com	www.rootsweb.com
Rough Guides	www.roughguides.com
Safekeeper Vest	www.safekeepervest.com
SeatGuru	www.seatguru.com
Seniors Home Exchange	www.seniorshomeexchange.com
SideStep	www.sidestep.com
Sister Cities International	www.sister-cities.org

Skype	www.skype.com
Snapfish	www.snapfish.com
SoloDining.com	www.solodining.com
Sony	www.sonystyle.com
Soundwalk	www.soundwalk.com
Southwest Airlines	www.southwest.com
Spa Finder	www.spafinder.com
SteriPEN	www.steripen.com
Tax Back International	www.taxbackinternational.com
Technorati	www.technorati.com
TerraPass	www.terrapass.com
Thomas Cook	www.thomascookpublishing.com
Time Out	www.timeout.com
TotalVid	www.totalvid.com
Trails.com	www.trails.com
Transportation Security Administration	www.tsa.gov
Travel Blogs	www.travelblogs.com
Travel Health Online	www.tripprep.com
Travel Photographers Network	www.travelphotographers.net
Travel Sentry	www.travelsentry.org
Travelocity	www.travelocity.com
TravelSmith	www.travelsmith.com
UNESCO	www.unesco.org
U.S. Department of State	www.travel.state.gov
U.S. Department of State Passport Information	www.iafdb.travel.state.gov
The Weather Channel	www.weather.com
Wellness Concierge	www.wellnessconcierge.com
WhichBudget	www.whichbudget.com
Wide World Books & Maps	www.wideworldtravels.com
Wi-Fi-FreeSpot	www.wififreespot.com
Wikitravel	wikitravel.org

World Alliance of YMCAs	www.ymca.int
World-Wide Opportunities on Organic Farms	www.wwoof.org
XE.com	www.xe.com
Zagat Survey	www.zagat.com

INDEX

Sunburn, 119

Tax refunds, 163–64
Taxis, 84–85
Tetanus, 121–22
Text messaging, 196
Theater, 25
Theft, luggage, 176–77
Tickets, paper, 59
Tipping, 163
Toilets, 122–23
Tours, group, 13–16, 22
Trains, 78–80
Transportation, 77–89
Transportation, local, 88–89
Travel warnings, 166
Travelers checks, 160
Travelers, meeting, 184–85
Trip, legnth, 48
Trip, timing, 48–49

Vehicles, paperwork, 95
Video, 151
Visas, 93–95
Volunteering, 21–22

Water, 112–13
Wildlife, 19
Work, 23–24, 35, 38

Yeast infection, 117
Yellow fever, 122
YMCAs, 72–73